# RELEASE FROM PHONINESS

# RELEASE
## FROM
# PHONINESS

by
**Arnold Prater**

WORD BOOKS, Publisher
Waco, Texas—London, England

# CONTENTS

# A WORD FROM THE AUTHOR

This book was born because of people.
They came to my office in the past few years in
substantial numbers. Others I met in the coffee
shops where businessmen gather for their breaks,
and still others sat in my congregations. Some I
met on jet planes, in airport waiting rooms and
highway cafes. There were others who brushed my
life at laymen's retreats and at ministers'
conferences where I spoke across the country.

Their questions were all the same: "How can I
find something real?" In great numbers they
were sick to death of the frantic, phony life
which saps at their spiritual bloodstreams and
drains their physical bodies until they are near the
breaking point. Many of them were leading
churchmen; others had left
the church and still others had never been
Christians at all. But without exception their
dilemma was the same. "Something's missing
and we've got to find it!"

In this book I have tried to give some answers—
not theories, but answers I see being lived out in

others and which I have found in my own quest. I have tried to put them in today's language. But they are not new. They are very, very old and—I am convinced—very, very true.

My purpose herein has been twofold: first, to point up the way out of the phony life; and second, to guide in what to do after one has found the Way.

Christian growth is the big problem for new or rededicated Christians. "What do I do next?" they ask. Joining a small prayer group in the church is not possible for many since there are none where they are. So for a while, at least, they must go it more or less alone. Here is what to do in the interim until one finds such a group or forms one himself.

Then there is another reason for this book: It is that after all these years of following Him who is the Way, I am still so excited about it I just *had* to put it down on paper!

What a great and glorious liberation awaits the sincere seeker when he finds that most exciting, thrilling, and wonderful thing that can happen to a human being when he stops living a lie!

# Chapter 1

## WHO NEEDS IT?

God is not a giant IBM card who comes sliding out of some colossal computer when you have pressed all the right buttons.

But you can find Him. You can be for real. You can be a new person. This is a book for the desperate, for only the desperate will truly seek God. Don't lay it down, though, simply because you think you are not desperate.

"I am not desperate," you may say. "Things are not too bad with me. It was only an idle curiosity that led me to this page."

Was it? Or was it perhaps the manifestation of a deep sense of inner dissatisfaction? One that seldom rises to the conscious level but which nevertheless appears from time to time?

In a sense almost everyone I meet is desperate. I don't mean they are panic-stricken. I don't mean their pulses are pounding with despair or that their hearts are racing as they frantically seek the big answers.

Most people are quietly desperate. Behind their masks and the novocaine smiles they don of a morning, there is a deep sense of uneasiness. They have become clever and adroit at putting it down, but still at some time during most every day the meaninglessness and the phoniness of their routine flits across their conscious minds and they think, "If only it could make sense. If only it were not 95 per cent pretense. If only I could escape from this stage on which I daily play out my role. If only . . . if only!"

They are the quietly desperate.

We are curious and terrible contradictions. Each of us wants to find God. Each of us want to be for real. Each of us wants to become a new person.

But everyone erects a wall of lies between himself and reality. Life is a process of removing the bricks from that wall so we can see clearly. There are some of those bricks we cannot remove by our own strength. We know that. We have sincerely tried, but they won't budge. We need help, big help.

Well, there *is* help. Big help. You *can* find God. You can become for real. You can become a new person. This I *know* and I know it for certain!

So almost everyone, in a sense, is desperate, either openly or quietly. But many want easy answers and there are none. You see, the symbol of the Christian faith is not a $69.50 platform rocker with a built-in vibrator. The symbol of our faith is a Cross and a cross is a painful, hurtful thing that always means ultimate death. Still many persist in seeking easy, pat answers. They want God in a giant economy-size box and at bargain prices.

One Sunday afternoon about 2 P.M. my phone rang. It was our church custodian saying there was a man in my office who had to see me at once. I was weary from the efforts of the morning but there was an urgency in his voice that would not be put off, so I went at once. I found in my office a transient wretch of a man—dirty, unshaven, red-eyed and ragged. He was obviously deeply under the influence of alcohol and he sat with his head in his hands, sobbing his heart out. When the custodian introduced me, the man looked up and, like a frightened, trapped animal, cried, "You're a preacher, aren't you? You're supposed to have all the answers—well, give me God!"

My heart churned with empathy for this poor creature who out of his despair and lostness thought I could just hand God to him and solve all his problems. And for a moment I wished with all my heart I could reach in my coat pocket and give him a neat little fliptop box, in which God, all transistorized and miniaturized, could be found.

God was there with us. God was as near to that wretched man as He was to me—and not many times in my life have I sensed so deeply the awful barrier human beings build between themselves and the One who wants to rescue them. But this man had erected a wall between himself and reality. He was desperate, but not yet willing to examine the price tag to victory.

Most of us have never reached this stage of physical depravity, and yet millions of persons live within the framework of the same principles of self-delusion and unreality which had snared this human derelict.

It is no trouble to spot the desperate ones among the down-and-outers. The hippies, those who ride the wild horses of LSD, the gaunt ones in the ghettos—these are all easy to see. But sometimes it is not just the down-and-outers who are desperate, sometimes it is the up-and-outers.

A college student sat in my office and said to me with a terrible earnestness, "What is the point in it all? If we are honest we are labeled and treated with contempt. The only way we can get along is to be phony like everybody else!"

A dynamic, successful executive with three cars and a beautiful home in the suburbs said to me, "I know it is all a fake. My business is based on buttering up people, feeding their egos. My fine home, speed boat, my cars, my two hundred dollar suits—these are all only the necessary props for making still more money." Now that he had found the courage to say it, he went on, "Even my marriage is a fake. My wife and I play roles for the sake of the children. There is nothing deep and honest and real!"

A young housewife confessed, "I feel like a squirrel trapped in a revolving drum. I run frantically all day long and get nowhere. I am not loved for what I am but only for what I do. If only I could find some meaning for these cocktail parties which my husband says I must attend for his sake! If only I could find some meaning in throwing clothes into the washer, or picking up toys strewn about the house, or going to wedding showers and parties!"

Over in India, gliding sluggishly across the bosom of the land like a great brown python is the Ganges river. It is muddy and filthy and filled with the garbage and human refuse from a hundred million people. But annually, thousands of the devout crawl on their bellies for

miles doing penance until they reach its slimy banks.
Then they wade out into it to their waists and lift their
hands heavenward and cry aloud. What are they doing?
They are seeking to make atonement for their own sins.
They are trying to find God. Life as they know it is one
day after another of hunger and small meaningless
rounds within the structure of their primitive society,
and they are desperately seeking sense and meaning to it
all. Through this ritual they hope to become new
persons.

"Holy men" there sit on beds of nails and stare at the
sun until their eyes become sunken sightless holes in their
heads. And why? Because they deeply sense that there is
something big and wonderful and meaningful to life as it
is given to us, but they haven't been able to find it, so
they seek it through self-mutilation.

In all honesty, what is the basic difference between
these people and the drunken, defeated man who sat in
my office? What is the basic difference between them
and the college student, the "successful" executive and
the young housewife? Down where life matters, most
are all identical. They want to find God. But they
have erected this wall of lies between themselves and
reality, and as long as that wall stands there they can
never find the healing they seek. Something is bugging
them and they cannot isolate it. They are bewildered
and mystified, seeking small answers for big questions,
cheap solutions for costly problems.

Do you fit in here somewhere? Of course you do. You
want to find God, you know you do. I am addressing the
desperate ones now, not only those who are openly frantic but those who deeply and quietly seek.

Is there an answer? Is there an answer for *you?* Of course there is an answer. If you are living in the shadows, stop and think. *There could be no shadows if there were not light somewhere!*

Before we begin to speak about the Light, let's go a bit further in this matter of symptoms. We human creatures are marvelously constructed, both physically and psychologically. When stress comes upon us we have innate abilities to compensate. If too much light attempts to enter the eye, the pupil will compensate by contracting and limiting the amount of light which can enter.

Psychologically, if we are thrown into patterns of neurosis or maladjustment the mind seeks to compensate. So some of the obviously desperate ones compensate for their fears and phoniness by drifting off into alcoholism. And under its influence the mind will reflect, during certain stages, great evidences of confidence, well-being, and outward self-assurance. Actually, of course, it is trying to compensate for the gnawing, deep fear, boredom, and sense of meaninglessness that is a deep reality within the person.

It is too easy and comfortable to single out the alcoholic. But his symptoms can be the same as ours. The only difference is that his symptom is the bottle while ours is something less condemned and more easily tolerated by society.

A little girl I know grew up in a home where God was not known. Consequently her parents' anxieties and frustrations and unhappiness in marriage were transmitted to her. She grew up mystified by this strange big world in which there was no place for her—no place where she could feel loved, wanted, and needed. She could not find God, for she had hardly heard of him. All she knew was that life did not seem to have meaning, and she was unable to see any value in herself as an individual. The one thing she learned from her parents was how to wear the mask. Outwardly, she became very clever at deceiving the world, but inwardly she was a seething mass of fears, resentments, and uncertainties.

By the time she was twelve years of age her weight reached one hundred and fifty pounds. At sixteen she weighed two hundred. Food became her compensation. She could find at the table a momentary interruption of the task of living in fear instead of the excitement of living in love. At the table she was trying to satisfy a much deeper hunger—a hunger to be free from meaninglessness, a hunger to feel loved and wanted, a hunger to find herself. Steak and sour cream became the substitutionary food for the Bread of Life. And because a substitute can never satisfy, she continued to eat long after her physical needs had been satisfied. The longer she ate, the longer she could maintain the illusion that she had found the answer at the table. This is not to say that everyone who is overweight fits into this category but only to illustrate how some *thing* can become a substitute for reality.

Work can become compensatory. I know the sad story of a minister who spent many years in the ministry. He was known as a sixteen-hour-per-day person. He was tireless and drove himself to the point of utter exhaustion every day. He was admired by his fellows and by his congregation for his zeal. But at the age of forty-five he suddenly resigned from the ministry and took a job in another area of work. He blamed others. He could obtain no cooperation from his congregation; his superiors did not appreciate his work. All the fault lay with others. He had attempted by sheer busyness to atone for the vacuum he knew was in his heart. He was one of the desperate ones. He was not for real, and deep down he knew it.

Sometimes people fall into the classification of those who "enjoy poor health." They drift off into one physical complaint after another in order to avoid facing up to the reality of their need.

Some have a need to gossip—to take a morbid interest in the affairs of others. They know all the latest scandals, the latest rumors, and are quick to speculate about the activities of others. These persons are almost always hypercritical. Negative criticism is the hallmark of their lives. This is compensatory. They must externalize their own inner conflicts in order that they might avoid reality.

Even church-going can become compensatory. (Please, don't let me discourage anyone from attending worship!) A long time ago I was pastor of a man who owned several shacks in the poorest part of town and who charged exorbitant rents. Yet he was one of the biggest givers to foreign missions we had. Was this compensatory? Did he seek to compensate for his lack of true commitment by being regular at worship and among the top givers?

So it is with the desperate. Somewhere I have read the phrase, "the happy pagans." It is not so. Our land is brimful of people who live out their lives in boredom, meaninglessness, and in spreading the illusion that they are happy by falling gaily into the pattern of the routine of the culture. They give the impression of gaiety, but there is no sparkle in their lives. Go downtown and take a look at the thronging crowd, away from friends and neighbors upon whom they must make an impression. How many happy faces does one see? When the mask is off, their faces are tired and lined and strained with the inner tensions with which they must struggle. They have found no real reason for living and have no real hope for dying.

Well, of course, the only question in the world that has any relevancy to what I have said thus far is simply this: What about *you*? In all of this, have you seen anything of yourself? Did you really begin to read this book out of mere curiosity, or do you need help? Are you really, down underneath it all, seeking for something you have not yet found? Or Someone? Are you actually weary unto death of all this phoniness, this role-playing, this false relationship to life and to yourself? Are you ready to say, "Yes, much of this fits me. I wish . . . I wish . . ."

If somewhere in this chapter you have not even caught the slightest gleam of something that resembles you, then this book is not for you. But if on the canvas of these pages there has been etched a faint something that resembles the true conditions of your life, then be glad you are one of the desperate ones, for you can be helped. God has some answers for you. You are ripe for finding that which you have been seeking. It is only those who feel no need whom God cannot help. For them, He must await another day.

But not for you. You see a need in your own life and you feel a sincere yearning to be freed from all this artificiality. So be glad! Give thanks! You are just about ready to take the first step.

And now I want to assure you—not that I have "arrived," not that I am in any sense superior to you, not that my needs are one whit different than yours, but simply because I have found sense and meaning to life. I want you to find it, too. Not as *I* have found it, but as God will reveal it to you.

I would not for the world say that what I am going to say in these pages is the only way to find God. God will make Himself known as He wills. I am not going to say that these pages hold the only secret of release from phoniness . . . but I will say with assurance that this way is *one* way. That I know. And my confidence springs from the kind of God we have. The kind that Jesus Christ revealed to us. The God of the second chance. The God who brought the creation out of chaos and who brings His creatures who are flattened by failure to a faith in Him and then gives them something with which to glue it tight to reality—even His love.

The God of a second chance.

In a lowly spot in England a young doctor was assigned to be in charge of a hospital. Later he was to become a famous author in his own right, but first he had to live awhile. He had not been there long when a boy about six years of age was brought in who had a severe case of diphtheria. The boy was even then gasping and choking and in a matter of moments his life would be gone. Even though he had never performed such an operation, the young doctor knew that only emergency surgery could save the child. So he performed a tracheotomy, an incision in the windpipe. He was assisted by a young girl who had received her degree in nursing only a short time before. With fear and trembling he began to work. It seemed to him the job would never end, but at last the operation was completed. He inserted a tube in the incision and the lad began to breathe without difficulty.

In the early hours of the morning he heard a loud pounding on his door. Opening it, he found the young nurse who had helped him. Hers had been the job of sitting up through the night to make certain the tube for breathing remained open. But though her spirit was willing, her flesh was weak and she too was exhausted from the strain of the surgery. She had fallen asleep, and while she was asleep, the tube became blocked and the boy had died.

The story goes that at this point the doctor lost his head and swore that she would have to pay for this and that he would certainly see that she was reported. After a while he called her into his office and read the report to her while she stood there trembling with fear and overcome with remorse and shame. When he had finished he said, "Well, have you anything to say?" She fearfully nodded her head and dared to look up and turn her tear-splashed face towards him. "Please, sir," she said falteringly, "give me another chance."

It had not occurred to the doctor that he might do this. It was all cut and dried so far as he was concerned. She had failed. Her mistake had cost a life. She must pay. It was just that simple.

But that night he could not sleep. He kept hearing her

cry, "Please give me another chance." All night he wrestled with the memory of that voice, and the Lord tormented him with reminders of mercy and compassion. The next morning he tore up the report.

Years later the young nurse went on to become head of a great children's hospital, loved by all, giving herself over and over again to children who needed her love and great heart. Suppose the girl had fled and not faced up to the wrong that was in her actions? Suppose the good doctor had not given her another chance? Ah, but that is idle speculation—for he did!

Well, would God do any less than he? The good doctor would be the first to deny this. He is a God of a second chance. That is why He exchanges prodigals' rags for purple robes of royalty. Because He is a God of beginning again.

And He shows us the way! The story is told that in a certain province in Japan many centuries ago, crops failed because of a drouth and that autumn famine was imminent. So the emperor decreed that all persons over the age of seventy years must be destroyed in order that the young might live through the winter.

Sorrowfully one young man in the village picked up his aged and weakened mother and began to search for a place in which he could take her life and bury her. He climbed slowly and painfully to the top of a high mountain to a clearing in the woods. He tenderly laid his mother upon the ground and rested for a moment before doing what he had been ordered to do.

"One thing, Mother," he asked, "Why did you keep tearing bits of your shawl loose as we came up to this place?"

And the weakened mother replied, "I wanted you to be able to find your way back down the mountain!"

Could God do this for us? Would God do this? Yes, precisely. We have made a mess of things. Famine has come into our lives. We even carried Him up a mountain outside an ancient city and there we crucified Him. But He has scattered some signs all along the way so we could find our way back to Him!

# Chapter 2

## HOW BADLY DO YOU WANT IT?

Like suddenly ignited gasoline, pride has a way of flaring up and building a flaming barrier between us and God.

This is what is very likely to happen when I tell you that the first step in finding God is the admission of failure. But there is no way around it. First of all we must come to admit that we have not really been able to cope with life—that our lives haven't turned out as we had hoped under our management.

No one will truly make this admission until he is desperate, either openly or quietly. This is why we emphasized it so strongly in the first chapter. God cannot break through to us until we have finished the futile game of trying to be the power behind our own lives.

No one likes to admit that he has failed. One can find all kinds of evidence that he is not a complete failure. But we need to be perfectly honest and ask ourselves a few questions. Am I satisfied with my own life as I know it? Am I content to go on just as I am? If I am not a failure, why am I concerned about being released from phoniness?

But I say again, God cannot change things until one is fully ready to accept the fact that life as he knows it is not satisfactory and that all his efforts to make it so have failed.

The story of self-reform is a sad one. We enter into a vicious cycle that begins with grim determination to change things. We sail along for a while and then deterioration sets in. Eventually comes the knowledge that we have failed again, and our dissatisfaction is compounded by the additional guilt feeling that once more we have tried and failed. Thus we end up worse off than we were before.

Jesus illustrated this with the Parable of the Seven Devils. When we throw out one of the demons which has been haunting us—while we are sweeping it out the front door—seven more enter via the back door.

Somewhere I heard the story of a farmer who was having trouble with a hawk which was preying on his chickens. So he set a trap for the bird, and one day he captured it. So elated was he that he decided to give the hawk a fitting punishment for its evil deeds. He tied a stick of dynamite to the leg of the bird, lit the fuse, and turned it loose. But instead of flying high into the air, the hawk flew into the farmer's barn, and the explosion blew up the barn.

In just this way all our high resolves and noble intentions come back to haunt us and destroy us when we try to go it alone.

You must admit failure. The Bible is filled with stories that verify this. Time after time it was only after Israel had admitted its failure that God was able to bless the nation once more.

The woman who was healed by touching the hem of the Master's robe had tried everything for eighteen years. She had spent all she had on one doctor after another, trying to help herself. It was only when, with a courage born of desperation, she came to Jesus that she was healed.

When the disciples were on the raging sea they did everything within their nautical knowledge to try and make shore safely. They pulled out all the stops; they used every trick in the book. At last it became perfectly obvious to them that all their efforts were in vain. Then it was that they called on the Lord and were saved. They were willing to do this only after they had to admit defeat.

Pride says, "Surely you are not that weak! Surely there is a way out. Don't give up yet!"

Pride says, "Look on the plus side of your life! Count all your blessings! See how you are respected in the community! How could you possibly admit complete defeat?"

But God says, "If my people who are called by my name shall humble themselves, pray, seek, crave and require of necessity my face, and turn from their wicked ways, then will I hear from Heaven, forgive their sin, and heal their land" (II Chron. 7:14, *The Amplified Bible*).

Let's reason this thing out. If we are so successful, why do we continue to feel this awful need to impress others? Why do we don the mask, many times even in the presence of our families?

There is a deep spiritual and a psychological law involved here: "He that would save his life shall lose it."

Alcoholics Anonymous has been wise enough to acknowledge this law which is woven tightly into the fabric of the universe. The very first step in their twelve step program of rehabilitation is this:

> We admitted we were powerless over alcohol—that our lives had become unmanageable.

If you want to be a real person, here is the starting place. Leave out the alcohol bit if it doesn't apply to you and say aloud, "My life has become unmanageable."

This is what the thief on the cross admitted. He had come to the end of his futile life. He had no other hope left. He admitted his need, and when he did this, God in Christ came crashing through into his life with victory.

But there were two thieves on the crosses that day. The second thief was identically situated with the first. All his attempts to run his own life were at an end. And yet, even when hope was gone, pride blocked the way. He'd show them how to die. He'd show them he could take it. He was the master of his fate. He was the captain of his soul. And he died a phony, an unreal person, without God.

This is what pride will do to us. Even as we stand in the charred ruins of our self-blackened lives, pride asks us to declare, "My house still stands!"

To whom do we admit our failure? First to ourselves and then to God. It is never easy to admit failure, but it is always easier to admit it to ourselves than it is to God.

Deep down we *know* we are not what we should be.

We know the true conditions that exist there, unless we have rationalized them into unimportance.

But if it is difficult to admit defeat to ourselves, it is even more difficult to admit it to God. Well, where will this admission take place? Why, it takes place at the same place the thief made his admission—at the *Cross of Jesus Christ.*

Remember the old hymn?

"At the Cross, At the Cross, where I *first* saw the light."

You see, if I said to you simply, "Admit your failure to God," this would confuse you. You'd try to think of God and the result would be unreal. For the only way you can think of God and make any sense is to think of Jesus. If you try to think of God without Him, all you get is either a bearded old man or a gray blob of psychedelic ectoplasm flitting from planet to planet, and both pictures are unreal.

The only way you can think of God and make any sense is to think of Jesus. And if you are seeking God, you seek Him through Jesus the Christ, and when you want to be released from your phoniness, when you want to become a new person, you seek Him at the place where the thief found Him—at the Cross!

So when I honestly face up to the Cross of Jesus Christ, when my ultimate confrontation with it comes, I face up to it by bowing down—by admitting my need, my failure, my powerlessness over life. I have to bow down and what is the truth? *I don't like to bow down* before anything or anybody! Oh, I do it—physically, I mean. I get down on my knees many times during the course of a year. But it is possible to bow down with the knees and not bow down with the heart.

There is a picture in my mind of a rebellious little boy. His mother has taken him downtown shopping. She wants to do a little errand by herself so she takes him to the lobby of a great hotel. She leads him to a chair and says to him, "Now, you sit in this chair until I return. I won't be very long."

She starts out the front door and, glancing back over her shoulder, sees the little boy sliding down out of the chair. She goes back and says, "Son, I told you to sit down!"

"But I don't want to sit down," he declares. So she forces him. He sits in the chair, and she starts for the front door once more. As she does, the little boy's cry rings out loud and clear across the lobby, "Mom, I'm sitting down—*but I'm standing up inside!*"

Standing up inside. Many times I bow down but I'm standing up inside. This is phony. This is unreal. This is faking it. But when I come squarely to the Cross of Jesus Christ, I *must* bow down for until I do bow down I'm not facing up.

I don't like to admit failure in running my own affairs. I don't like to bow down at the Cross because when I do, I must take off my mask. I really don't want to remove my mask. It is much more comfortable with it on. But I must . . . for you cannot face God wearing a mask!

You do not fool God. Adam and Eve tried it; they disobeyed God and, when they did, the Amplified Bible says, "Then the eyes of them both were opened and they knew that they were naked . . ." (Genesis 3:7). At least one meaning of this is that when they saw their nakedness uncovered, that is, when they saw clearly they were disobedient children of God, the thought struck them that he would be paying them a visit that evening. They realized what they had done so they began to put on clothing. They began to seek a mask to try and cover their disobedience. They couldn't hide it from themselves but they tried to hide it from God. But God was not fooled.

And when I bow down, when I admit my defeat and failure, that which I knew all the time, I have to discard my pretense, my sham, my phoniness and self-delusion, because God cannot tolerate masks.

Further, if we will not remove our masks voluntarily, inevitably life itself will remove them for us, because this is the way existence is arranged. Sooner or later the moment of truth comes and God takes off our masks.

When they crucified the Son of God, the earth trembled in protest and the veil of the temple was rent. And remember, it was split from *top to bottom,* not from bottom to top. This was God's way of saying that he doesn't approve of masks.

At Calvary God ripped off the mask of human nature and exposed it for what it truly is—an ugly, hateful, self-seeking thing which will stop at nothing in its attempt to have its own way.

So now you have come seeking God. You have come to the only place you can find Him, at His Cross. But even here there is danger. Even here the old attempt at self-sufficiency is likely to make one last effort to assert itself. You see, we have become so clever at fooling other people, it is perfectly natural for us to try and make one last effort to deceive God.

We see Him hanging there and we cry out, "Who did this terrible thing to you, Jesus? Was it the Jews? Was it my neighbors? Was it all the cruel and thoughtless people who live in my town? Tell me, who put you there? I'll take care of them!"

You see, I'm wearing my mask, I want him to think I'm on *His* side. But He knows better, and through His pain-clenched teeth He says to me, "You did it, my son, it was you!"

Who, me? When He says this, it breaks by heart. Oh, how it hurts me, because I don't want anybody to suffer on account of me. I never intended to hurt anyone with my little habits, or my sharp tongue. I didn't want to crucify anybody with my shoddy talk or my neglect of the needs of other people.

I had no intention of causing this through the resentment I harbored towards that relative who wronged me, or that man who got my promotion, or by prejudices to which I had clung for years. I wanted all that to be strictly *my* business. But now I have come to admit my failure in managing my own life, I have come to the Cross to find God and He tells me very pointedly that I am the one who put Him there.

So my reaction (you see, this is how I have handled my mistakes all my life) is to cry out, "Oh Christ, let me make it up to you! I promise I'll do better. I'll read my Bible more, I'll pray a lot more, I'll increase my pledge to the church, I'll attend worship more regularly, you'll see . . . I'll make it up to you Lord, you'll see!"

Thus I make my promises to Him. When it really hits

me that my phoniness and my unreality has not only made life unbearable for me, but it has crucified the Son of God, I say everything I can think of to Him—everything except the *one thing* He wants me to say. For it is truly a difficult thing for me to say to Jesus Christ, "I'm sorry!" It is much easier for me to make rash promises and form creditable resolutions than it is to say, "I'm sorry," and truly mean it.

For the truth of the matter is that I am *not* sorry. I still don't want to give up. I don't want to relinquish my sins. The raw truth is that there are some of my sins I *like*. How can I say I am sorry about it all when this stark fact is imbedded firmly within?

It is prefectly obvious to me that the only way I can really be honest here at the Cross is if something happens within me to change some of my likes to dislikes. I have tried to change this myself. I have tried to cease liking some of the things I know I shouldn't, but I have failed every time. Why, it would take a *miracle* for me to be changed like this!

Now, if I am truly in earnest, if my desperation is genuine, this is *precisely* what is about to happen!

I see my need, and now I am ready to admit it. I long ago admitted it to myself; now I am ready to admit it to God. Ready to admit that life has finally proven to be too much for me. And the mess I have made of it up to now is entirely of my own making.

An ancient story is told of a smithy in the Middle Ages who took a great pride in his work. He placed his mark on everything that came from his shop, for he wanted people to know of his great skill and prowess at the forge. His country went to war and the invading army conquered the city in which the smithy lived. He was captured and thrown into irons. Secretly he knew that he could escape for he knew all about chains. He knew that in most all of them there was a weak link and that night he planned to find it and break the chains with his mighty strength. But when darkness came and he felt for the weak link his fingers ran across a mark on one of the links. It was his own mark! And his heart sank in despair for he knew there were no weak links in his chains. He had taken too much pride in his own work, and now he was hopelessly trapped by the very thing he had forged.

I, by my own choosing, have made my life exactly what it is up to this point, and now I've got to have help. I admit it.

Why does God ask that I come to this point? Why does God ask me to discard all this phoniness and unreality and admit that I cannot cope with life by myself?

Is He a bit on the sadistic side? Is He trying to prove to Himself that He is the Lord of all? Must He prove anything to Himself? Is He a sort of a proud old executive-type gentleman who must have His ego flattered? Is this the kind of a God He is? Why is it so vital and necessary that I be prostrated and humiliated before Him?

No, our God is not a sadist; He does not have to prove anything to Himself about His own power; He doesn't have to have His ego flattered; He doesn't *have* an ego in the sense that we do. He doesn't demand obeisance like some senile monarch.

God requires us to come to this point for one reason and one reason only, for *only in this way is He able to do what He wants to do for us.*

God has given you and me a great and terrible thing in the gift of our freedom of choice. And as long as we hold something back, just that long is God hindered from doing for us what He wants to do—what needs to be done. For He will not wrestle any area of our lives from us if we choose not to let go.

God never arbitrarily withholds good things from His children. "If ye then, being evil, know how to give good things unto your children, how much more will your Father which is in heaven give good things to them that ask him?" (Matthew 7:11 KJV). God did not withhold penicillin from the human race arbitrarily. It did not please Him to see little children die of pneumonia; but He *had* to wait until the race developed to the point where a man like Sir Alexander Fleming *chose* to lend his mind to study and research with sufficient perception that God could bestow the gift. Similarly, He does not withhold the life free from unreality and phoniness because He is capricious or arbitrary. He wanted to grant this release a long time before we finally came to the point where we would choose to let Him do it. And this point begins precisely at the time we become willing to admit that we can go no further without Him, that we cannot run our lives by ourselves, that we are incapable of coping with life by our own wits. As long as we insist in seeking to give the impression to others that everything is just fine and dandy with us, as long as we insist on donning the mask of icy, antiseptic impeccability, just that long are God's hands tied.

Herein lies a great trouble in the church. Churches over this land are filled with men and women who bear the label of Christian, but who insist on running their own lives. They have done well in the world and the world knows it. The status symbols and signs abound in their lives, the community respects them, and many of them have responsible places of leadership. But pride has replaced humility and they no longer feel the need to be "driven to that grace which makes the wounded whole." Can you imagine very many leading churchmen who would stand and pray in all earnestness, "God be merciful to me, a sinner?" We need to come again to the Christian perspective that sees us as objects of God's grace, love, and mercy.

To admit we need help is the first step towards wholeness. Take another look at the Prodigal Son. Here he is lying out in the hogpens of life. He thought he could make it on his own. He needed help from no one, thank you. He could manage very well by himself. He had assets, and everyone knows that's what it takes in this world.

But where has this course landed him? Squarely at the point of failure. He could have stayed there, dirty, starving, and miserable, insisting right up to the end, "I'll find a way out of this somehow." He still had his freedom of choice. No one was forcing him to decide anything.

But where does the miracle part of this wonderful story begin? It begins at the point of *admission*.

The Amplified Bible says:

> Then when he came to himself, he said, how many hired servants of my father have enough food and to spare, but *I am perishing* (dying) here of hunger! [Italics mine]
> ( Luke 15:17)

Here is where the admission part of the story begins, "I am perishing." Until he admitted his plight, the only thing that happened was that things kept getting worse. Until he began to be honest with himself and see things as they really were, there was nothing that could be done for him. His father was waiting for him in the warm, comfortable house, but he could not go to the hogpens and force the stubborn boy. Had he done so, the boy's rebellion would only ultimately have increased.

But the Prodigal began to take stock. Then he makes the next admission:

"I will get up and go to my father and I will say to him, Father, *I have sinned* against heaven and in your sight; *I am no longer worthy* to be called your son . . ." [Italics mine]
Luke 15:18-19

How the admission of failure rolled out of him! And the miracles began to happen from that point on. His pride took a long, wistful look at the future and fell dead at his feet.

Now, what about you? Is it worth it? Are you sick enough of the phoniness under which you have been living? How much more will it take? Have you had enough? What would it be like to sleep once more in the warm, wonderful beds of the Father's house?

This unreal existence in which you have been telling yourself that God doesn't really matter except when the baby gets sick or someone in the family dies, this gay Halloween atmosphere of pretense which seems to have caught up the entire family into its giddy, fake atmosphere of living—have you had enough? Do you want to be released from all this? Freed from the greedy, grasping tendrils of a life that has brought only a lonely, meaningless, boring, frustrating state of affairs? Are you ready to come to God on his terms, not yours? This thing which happened at Calvary has come rolling across twenty centuries, and like a surgeon's knife, pierces this present moment, this present second in our lives, with a shattering relevancy. Despair takes a look at Christ and, like a babe fresh born, utters a faint cry of hope. And that faint cry is the beginning of the miracles of a new life.

This admission is not easy. The Cross was not easy. But it is a strange thing—this very admission of your need will become the very unshakable foundation for all the wonderful things that are going to happen later on.

A combat crew had to ditch their bomber in the vast loneliness of the south Pacific ocean. Five of them climbed aboard a rubber raft and the rest were lost. For twelve days they drifted with no sign of rescuers. The hot, terrible heat from the sun scorched and burned their skin, and as their rations were exhausted their flesh shrank until they were little more than living skeletons. Their lips cracked and their tongues became thickly swollen with thirst. Two of the men went mad and leaped overboard. Another died quietly and they rolled his body into the sea. Only two were left. When a rescue vessel found the raft, only one man survived and when he had regained some strength he told of the death of his last companion.

"The night before you found us," he said, "it rained and the raft caught a pail of fresh water. I tried to give some to my buddy. It would have saved his life."

The airman's shoulders shook with sobs and it was a moment before he could continue.

Then he said, "But his mind was wandering and he had the idea that I was trying to give him sea water to poison him and finish him off . . . and he wouldn't drink . . . I was too weak to force him."

Then the airman cried and beat his pillow in frustration and said, "Oh, if only he had drunk the water I offered him . . . he could have lived!"

There is One who stands today saying to men and women everywhere and perhaps to you, "Whoever drinks of the water that I shall give him will never thirst; the water that I shall give him will become in him a spring of water welling up to eternal life."

But first one has to admit he needs it!

# Chapter 3

## YOU ARE HEALED OF BLINDNESS!

Sometimes a fierce tornado of life will come buzzing in and rip to shreds in a single instant the brave structure of lies we have built between ourselves and God. But more often than not our Christian growth is a matter of seeing that structure erode through the experiences we have which seek to teach us that His way is the only way.

You have made a decision. You have made the first step in becoming a new person, in obtaining release from phoniness. You have admitted your need. It has been difficult. Perhaps it has been the most difficult thing you have ever done in your life up to now, to admit in all candor and honesty: "Lord, in spite of appearances, in spite of everything I could find to the contrary, the truth is I have made a mess of things. I can no longer manage my life by my own power. I admit it. I need help, big help. I need it now!"

When a person who has been electrocuted by life becomes numb enough to his own pride to do this, he is already halfway home!

So now you are ready to go on. When you boil all the sins in the world down, there is really only one, and that

37

is the worship of the self. This is what the Bible is all about. Pick out any character, any story which tells of the failure of a person or persons; dig your way down to the bottom motive and you will find lurking there in the depths the dark sinister figure of the self. Just name a few to test my statement. Begin with Adam and Eve; go right on through with Cain, Joseph's brothers, King Saul, Jonah, Herod, Judas Iscariot, Ananias and Sapphira, and the ruler Agrippa. All were vicitims of the same sin—the worship of the self.

The Bible, of course, is not just the story of these people; it is the story of *every* person. It is the story of the lengths to which God was willing to go to give every person victory over this destroyer. Reduced to its simplest terms, salvation means to be saved *from* the self, *for* God. To put it in modern terms, as long as we are worshippers of the self we are phonies. We are not attached to reality, we live the big lie. And this is what we are dealing with in our quest. Release from the unreal.

Why do we worship the self? One reason is that we do not see it as it really is. If we could truly see that self of ours as it really is, we certainly would declare a holy war against our enslavement to it.

To use a homely illustration, suppose we received a beautiful package through the mail. It is beautifully and artistically gift-wrapped. We set it on the table and our family inspects it with "ohs" and "ahs" as they admire its beauty. It excites the admiration of friends and neighbors who drop by. It truly is a work of art and one thinks surely there never was a package like this. And then we open it and recoil in horror for inside the box is a poisonous snake, alive and wriggling. We would know then that whoever sent this package, so beautiful on the outside, was not our friend, but a deadly enemy.

The reason so many people try to live life on an unreal basis is because they have left the package of self sitting on the table, where its beautiful wrappings can be admired by all who see it. Many never open the package. If they did, they would be shocked to discover what the package was all about.

This is what we are about to do. We are going to open the package. We are going to tear off the artificial, the tinsel, the wrappings, the artistic arrangement of ribbons. We are going to look at the thing inside the box. And let me warn you it is a shocking experience.

We are going to confront ourselves. And we are going to do something we have never done, we are going to confront ourselves *objectively*.

Most people will never do this. This is because they have formed a beautiful image of themselves. They are "pretty nice people." There isn't anything really very bad about them. They are pleasant, friendly, likeable persons. Actually, people would admire them and appreciate them more if they really knew just how nice they are.

This is the image we build up about ourselves, and we project it, as best we can, onto everyone we meet, especially those whom we would impress. We become very adroit and clever in our techniques for doing this. We know just how to flash the winning smile, just how to give the firm, hearty handshake. We know how to conduct a good conversation by insisting that we talk about the things in which *they* are interested. We know just when to slip in the subtle word of flattery. Oh, we know how to get the things we want from other people, because this is the whole idea. We don't waste very much time on those who cannot be of use to us, and our circle of friends is very carefully cultivated from the standpoint of what they can do for us.

We have long ago rationalized this by concluding that this is how life is and this is what we must do and since we are doing pretty well, we must be a pretty fair sort of a person. The evidence that we are consists in the things of comfort which we have been able to acquire. Thus the masquerade becomes complete and we begin to believe that we really *are* this kind of a person—a "right guy"— and if we haven't had quite the success we had hoped for, it is only because the world has not yet learned to know and appreciate us.

This is the *subjective* image of ourselves which we have formed. Never once in our entire lives have we backed away from ourselves and taken a long, hard honest look *objectively*. When we do, we are apt to be horrified!

Early in my ministry I bought a tape recorder as a tool to help me in my profession. Do you remember the very first time you ever heard your voice on a tape recorder? Of course you do. I well remember when it happened to me. I was astonished, incredulous, and utterly shaken. My reaction was exactly the same as yours, "That simply cannot be me!" But it was!

All my life up until then I had always thought I had a round, resonant, smooth, pleasing, and well modulated voice. I mistakenly thought that it must be a pleasure for people to listen to me. But *this* sounded like a refugee from the Andy Griffith show! This character dropped his "r's," he slurred most of his syllables, he split his infinitives and "uh'd" and "ah'd" almost interminably. This simply couldn't be me! But it was.

What had happened? You see, all my life I had been listening to my voice from the *inside*. Now, for the very first time, I was listening to it from the outside. I was, for the first time, hearing my voice objectively. Hearing it as other people had been hearing it for years. *They* knew how I sounded to them, and now I knew, and when I realized it for the first time it really shook me up.

In just this manner we are going to take a long, hard objective look at the self we really are, not the image in which we pretend. And I promise you that it is a devastating experience. We are going to see ourselves from the outside.

Here is the starting place, *"What do I do to other people?* How do they see me? How do they go away thinking about me? What did I do to that man at the service station who filled my car with gasoline? What did I do to my children the last time I corrected them? What did I do to the persons to whom I've talked on the telephone today?"

Now do something tangible. Something definitely physical. Take pencil and paper and make a list of every person whose life has touched yours in the past twenty-four hours. Write down the name, the place and a brief comment about each one. *What did I do to them?* Back off from yourself and look objectively. Oh, how people need to see themselves as others see them!

I am thinking of a poor woman I knew many years ago. She was a chronic complainer. I know now that she was only issuing forth her own inner pain, but I didn't realize it then. She would call me regularly once a week to complain. There was something about the church she didn't like. Why didn't the custodian pick up the trash in the churchyard, and she had noticed some dust on the pews. The Boy Scouts had been in the church kitchen again and broken a glass. Why hadn't I been to see Mrs. So and So? She didn't like the service last Sunday, people were unfriendly, or the choir was sharp or flat, the organ was too loud or too soft and the sermon was too long or too short or too deep or too shallow and on and on and on, *ad infinitum—ad nauseam!*

This woman had named the name of Christ as her Saviour. Yet she had never confronted herself. It was a sick and needy self. It didn't get that way in an instant. It had been carefully nourished and fed for years. If she had been able to back away and view herself objectively —if she had honestly asked the question, "What do I do to other people?"—I am sure she would have fallen to her knees and cried, "God be merciful to me!"

Confront yourself. This is a step away from phoniness, from the unreal. When we tear open the package and see what is inside, we know that we didn't receive this package from a friend. The source from which this came did not have our well-being in mind nor our being well.

Who could worship a self like this? When Paul was describing the battlefield of the human soul he had just taken an objective look at himself and thus at all mankind. And when he saw what was inside the package he cried:

> O unhappy and pitiable and wretched man that I am! Who will release and deliver me from (the shackles of) this body of death?
>
> Romans 7:24 (Amplified Bible)

Perhaps you have begun by now to erect defenses. Perhaps you are beginning to think, "But surely I am not *all* bad." Of course you are not all bad. Nobody is. You are made in the image of God and many of his attributes are stamped in you. If you were entirely bad you would not have read this far in this book. You would have no desire to escape from the false life in which you have found yourself. There would be no desire welling up within you to change. You have admitted you need help and this itself is ample proof that you are worth helping.

But do not fall into the trap of justifying the self. The self is a master of deception. Over the years it has developed defense mechanisms that can convince you black is white if you listen subjectively. But we are backing away from that self and looking at it for what it really is. You are not seeking to improve yourself. Your goal is not to be better but to be *new!*

And this is the promise I am holding out to you. You *can* be for real. You can find God. You can be released from phoniness. You can become a new person.

But we have not finished. We must dig deeper into this matter of objectivity viewing ourselves, of seeing ourselves as others see us.

Confront yourself in order to establish your true identity. Thank God our blessed Lord never asked us to do a thing he didn't first do himself. When he went out into the wilderness to be tempted for forty days and nights he confronted himself. Read again of his temptations. They were all to worship the self. He confronted himself, which is only another way of saying he sought for and found his true and real relationship to the world; and when he came down off the mountain he was no longer to be known as a carpenter from Nazareth, but as Jesus, the Son of God.

The disciples gathered in the upper room and "tarried" there for six weeks. I am convinced they were confronting themselves. They were seeking to establish their true relationship with life and with the world, and when with "one accord" they gave themselves to God, the Holy Spirit came upon them and they got up and went out into the world to blow the roof off of despair.

John Wesley confronted himself. This little man, trained and blessed with the degrees and honors of that day, found that life was empty and meaningless for him, and he began the long journey to find his true purpose and relation to life and to the world. He later admitted that he was "proud in spirit" and more than a bit impressed with himself. But one night, when he had finally admitted his utter failure to be the master of his life, he confronted himself in a little meeting on Aldersgate Street in London, and there he became a new person. When the confrontation was past he felt his heart "strangely warmed," forgiven, blessed, and transformed.

He went out into the world and one bitterly cold night in northern England the mob came and pounded on his door until they broke it down. They stripped his clothing from him and smeared hot tar on his body and pasted feathers to it. They dragged him to the edge of the town and left him for dead.

But he came to and found a friend and cleaned himself up. The next morning he stood on a great stone by the side of the road in the gray of the freezing dawn as the miners trudged to their dreary jobs in the mines, and he cried out to them as they passed.

And what did he cry? "This is the coldest, most un-feeling group of people I've ever known?" No. "If you people appreciated me you wouldn't have treated me in this manner?" No. Instead, this little man, still stiff and sore from the beatings of the night before, cried at the top of his voice, "Harlots, beggars, thieves! To you I come with glad tidings!"

You see, he was no longer the learned don from Oxford, he was no longer the pious missionary from Georgia, he was a *new person!* He was for real, no longer a phony masquerading up and down the avenues of life, simply because he had become honest and objective enough to admit his need and confront himself; and in confronting himself, he found God in Christ.

Remember, we are opening the beautiful package which has been sitting on the table of your life for so long and so much admired and coveted by you. Are you ready to go on?

Take again your paper and pencil and begin to write. Go back to your early childhood for a starting place. Begin to think of every thing you ever did which deposited a feeling of guilt within you—every word spoken, every little secret incident of which you are ashamed. Cover it thoroughly; leave nothing out. Be ruthless; bring it back out into the open.

Come to your teenage years; pour it all out on paper. You need not describe in detail, only make notes which will recall the incident to your mind.

Delve into every incident that involved your secret life, tear it out, root it up, and bring it to life there on paper. Go on into your adult life. Was I demanding of my wife or husband? Remember every argument and look for the part you played. Are there lies there in my past? Have I deliberately used other people in my life to my own advantage with no thought of their feelings? Who are they? At what points have I felt frustrated? Who has hurt my feelings? Why were my feelings wounded? Was it because of pride? Look at your failures, the things you had hoped to attain. Who can I blame? At what points where I should have taken responsibility did I shirk it? What were the disciplines I lacked? What have I done to other people? What have I done to my family? How do they think of me? Do they constantly see me at my worst? What kind of an example have my children seen in me?

If you are a churchman you might ask: What has been my relationship to the church? Have I really tried to make a contribution to it by my service? Have I been critical of it without offering constructive suggestions? Have I used the church to improve my business image in the community? What are my true motives?

Do I hold resentment in my heart against anyone? What is the *real* reason? You can make your own list. You don't need my help. However, make it complete. But this one last question you must not omit—*What do I really want most from this life?* To find the true answer to this, your major drives and past actions will be all the proof you need.

Now right at this point some will say: "I see no need for opening all these old wounds afresh. This is a morbid and depressing thing and I will have nothing to do with it." Others might say: "I can bypass this. It isn't necessary." If this is your reaction, then you are not quite ready to be helped. There is still a bit of pride left; the self is still in command.

I would not ask you to do something I had not already done. I have done this in my own life, and, as I have previously said, it is a shattering experience. But when one does this spiritual exercise in an objective manner, it is surprising to state that, even as one at last acknowledges the fountain of his guilts, it is a vast relief to be able to bring them out into the open and look them squarely in the eye. We are not going to do this every day. I earnestly hope you will enter into it with all your heart. Be thorough, be complete, be honest.

Confront yourself. Open up the package and see if the thing you find in it is the thing you want to worship. See if it is the thing to which you want to devote the rest of your life.

Do not read further until you have done this one tangible, physical thing I have suggested. Lay the book down and come back to it later. It may take only a few hours for you to complete this or it may take two or three days. But above all things, be honest. Don't allow rationalization to enter in. Remember your voice in the tape recorder; stand off and take a true look. Open the package now.

Now the thing is done. You have had a long clear look at what was in the package. What you saw there was not the image of the kind of person you thought you were. You have just had a first hand look at the thing which nailed Jesus Christ to the Cross.

It was not the Temple crowd and Judas and Pontius Pilate and the soldiers who did it. It was human sinfulness that did it. It was the cult of the worshippers of the self. The Temple crowd and the rest just happened to be in that particular geographical and historical setting. It could have happened in India or Europe or South America, given similar conditions and conflicts. It could still happen today in Cairo, Brussels, Hong Kong, New York or in the city where you live. As far as this cult is concerned nothing has changed. Only the props have been altered. The stage is the same. It is still true today that if you live enough like Jesus you are going to get into trouble.

But now you have confronted yourself objectively and you have not liked what you found there. You certainly would not want to worship this self or set it up as a ruler to whom you would like to be subjected the rest of your life. You are feeling pretty humble, but strange to say, you are not feeling one bit discouraged. You'd think that one would feel completely and utterly hopeless after seeing what you have seen. But you don't feel that way. In fact, you probably have already begun to know a sense of liberation. What a relief to have off the disguise! The play is over and you are ready to shed all these escape devices which have had you bound for so long.

Now I want to tell you what to expect just a bit further down the road. A long time ago I knew a man who stood behind the second chair in a barber shop where I was a customer. The owner of the shop was a friend of mine, but this fellow in the second chair, a man of about sixty-five years of age, was about the vilest, most vulgar, profane, wicked-talking man I have ever known. He must have had some kind of fixation about preachers for it seemed to me that every time I entered the shop he doubled his output.

One day when I went in he was gone. I asked my

friend where he was, and my friend said, "Oh, he's been desperately ill. And for a while they despaired of his life."

Perhaps six weeks after that, as I was entering the Post Office one day, I heard a faint voice call my name. I turned and saw the profane man. He was seated in a car. Someone had driven him uptown and parked the car so he could watch the people pass. He was a mere shadow of a man and his face was the color of death itself.

He crooked a bony finger at me and I walked over to where he was. He said, in a voice so weak I had to lean forward to catch the words, "Preacher, I want to tell you something."

Then he went on, "I was in a coma down there in the hospital. I could not move nor see. They did not know it, but I could still hear, and I heard the doctor tell my wife, 'I don't think he can last another hour.' "

Then his voice trembled so it was a moment before he could continue. "Preacher," he said, "I had never prayed in my entire lifetime but I prayed then. I said, 'O God, if there is a God, I need you now!' and when I said that —I-I don't know how to put it in words, but all I can say is—I was given an assurance that He was there!"

Then the tears welled up in his reddened eyes and he said, "Oh, preacher, just imagine! I've kicked Him in the face every day of my life for sixty years, and the first time I called His name—*He came!*"

# Chapter 4

## THE MASK COMES OFF!

Relinquishment is the photoelectric cell which swings open the door to our lives so that God can come in. With our wills we cross the beam (barrier) which has kept the door shut.

God is nearer than the latest beat of your heart. It has never been his reluctance, but yours, that has kept you apart. Now your extremity, the desperation which caused you to admit your need, may have given him the first real opportunity to rescue you.

You want to be freed from the phony life, you want to be liberated from the awful necessity of living a lie, and you have already made two decisions. You have decided to admit your utter inability to manage your own life by yourself, and you have decided to be honest and confront yourself objectively. Do you realize you have already begun to divorce your life from the false and attach onto reality?

When we come to this point in our flight from phoniness, there is a stirring passage in the Psalms which describes us perfectly:

50

O Lord, the God of my salvation, I have cried to
You for help by day; at night I am in your presence.
    Let my prayer come before You and (really) enter
into Your presence; incline Your ear to my cry!
                          Psalm 88:1-2 (Amplified Bible)

We don't as yet know exactly how to do it, but we have
now reached the place where we must turn our lives
*completely* over to Christ. We have sadly viewed the results of what happens when we run on our power. Now
we must hook onto his power.

Remember the tape recorder? Let's look at it again.
How does it work? I speak into a microphone, and the
recording head, by rearranging the electromagnetic
molecules in the tape, faithfully fixes what I have said.

Then I play it back. Of my own free will I have chosen
what I will speak into the microphone. Now I hear re-
produced precisely what I wanted. But when I hear it, it
doesn't sound as I had hoped. I wasn't able to put into
words exactly what I meant. Furthermore, I made some
foolish mistakes in grammar which were not apparent to
me at the time. I thought I was doing a good job, but it
turns out that I have made a mess of it so I decide to try
again.

First, however, I must erase what has already been
recorded, that bumbling stumbling mess that resulted
even though I started out with good intentions. I spoke
the words onto that tape of my own free will and now I
want to erase them. So I say to the tape, "Words, be
erased!" I put them there with my voice, so they should
disappear at the command of my voice. *But they don't.*

I cannot talk them off, I cannot wish them off, I cannot wash them off. I cannot go away for awhile and come

back later and find they have faded away. Like Pilate of old I find that "what I have written, I have written."

Now, you do not have to be an engineer to know what is required to erase the words from that tape. All you have to do is re-run the tape through the machine, only this time you have pressed a switch, and the tap contacts the erasing head which is connected directly with the power source, a power *much greater* than that tiny little current which flowed from the microphone when I recorded the words.

I do not have to hit you over the head to pound home the application of this illustration. For by now you know full well that you cannot erase the old self which you worshipped for so long. You have admitted that. But there is a Power, a much greater Power, Who can destroy that old self and replace it with a new self. His name is Jesus Christ. When I decide to erase the tape and press the switch, the Power does the rest.

You are about to turn your life completely over to that Christ. There is another way to make the picture clear. Since we are thinking in the field of electricity, let's use it to paint another picture.

Here is the huge, indescribable complex wiring system in a great city. There are millions of wires in that city, a network so intricate and vast that a billion spiderwebs would be simple when compared to it. Wires run everywhere. Each building has its own extremely complicated maze of wires. Some are underground, some are overhead. They are attached to great generators, air conditioners, electric shavers, typewriters, computers—the list is endless. Then, of course, there are rooms in every home, each of which is filled with bulbs for light.

And naturally, somewhere there is the source of all this city's power. Into the city it flows. That power flows along every inch of that tremendous system with which the city is wired. There is not an inch of wire where that power is missing. To some places it flows automatically and constantly. To other places it flows, controlled by environmental commands ordered by thermostats, and at yet other places it flows into a switch.

As long as that switch is not on the power is withheld. Even though the rest of the city is operating smoothly, where the switch is not on, the power withholds itself. Someone has to turn on the switch.

Now suppose you are in that city. You are somewhere in the heart of it, surrounded by all this power system, but you sit in a dark room. You cannot see. If you were to try to walk in the darkness you would stumble and fall. The power is there in the circuit, but both the decision and the act are up to you. If you want light you must turn on the switch, complete the circuit, fulfill the conditions, and *then* the light will come.

Now, I have no wish to oversimplify this matter. I said in the very first sentence of this book that you do not find God simply by pressing all the right buttons. All word pictures fall short of truth and are imperfect, but we cannot do without them, for only by them can we see truth. There is a tremendous difference between flipping a switch and the complete yielding of the human will to God.

A little boy will pile up some dirt and say, "See my mountain!" But he has not captured the majesty and the grandeur of the Canadian Rockies. All he has done is to illustrate the general structure of a mountain in a very,

very small way. But if we do not know about mountains, the little pile of dirt helps.

Now we are ready to help you yield your life to God. How to do it is a thing that puzzles many people. Again we turn to a word picture. When a baby is born there is a sense in which the first thing the child must do is surrender to the air about it. For nine months it has been sustained by something that could not sustain it indefinitely. Now it must yield to the air or turn blue and die. It must begin to breathe.

You are about to be born a second time. The difference between you and the infant is that this time you must give your consent. The first time you had nothing to say about it, this time you have everything to say about it.

When you were born the first time you had no will in the matter; now you do. Just as the baby made a once-and-for-all commitment to the air, so now you make a once-and-for-all commitment of your life to God. You have a free choice in the matter, so you exercise that free choice. It is an act of your will. You relinquish that to him. You lift up that ugly self that you have discovered, and in effect you say, "Lord, here, take this thing, all of it, I give it all to you. I want to be rid of it completely."

Now, the human will is a much maligned thing. You have tried acts of the will before and failed. But the reason you failed was that you held your problems up like a target on a rifle range and peppered them with the bullets of your will, and they bounced off harmlessly. Your will was your rifle. The difference is that now you hand God the rifle! Let Him deal with the problem of your life. It's His responsibility.

You see, you have become *willing*. Isn't that a vastly

different you than the old one you know so well? The old
you was never willing to come this far. Already the first
miracle has happened.

To a person who has been living within the vast stream
of secularism this step may seem "impractical." And because of so many disillusionments in the matter of will-
power, he may be inclined to back away and begin to
hesitate, doubt, and question. He may begin to fear failure.

You want to be a real person? Well, what is the reality? The reality is that being stopped by the fear of failure is like going suddenly blind, there exists only the
blackness of no alternatives. The reality is that yielding
to the absolute Lordship of Jesus Christ is like seeing the
sun burst through the black clouds. Suddenly life is a
sun-drenched valley of possibilities. The reality is that
one becomes like Ebenezer Scrooge in Dickens' *Christmas
Carol*—you wake up from your dreamlike phony past,
and the enchanting realization comes upon you that God
has given you a second chance! You are no longer flattened by failure but fortified with faith!

But now a few last-ditchers will voice the final complaint, "Yes, but be specific! How *can* I turn my life over
to God?"

Here for the first time we come to something very simple. So simple that a child of ten can do it. All that is
needed is a *beginning!*

In this phony, transistorized, fliptop-box culture of
ours there are millions of people faking out their lives
because they will not do this one thing, make a start!

The scripture calls Jesus "the finisher" of our faith,
but nothing can be finished unless it is first begun.

One day a lady who has charge of the communionware in our church came into my office. She had lost the key to the cabinet where it was kept. We had a board filled with duplicate keys to various parts of the building but for the life of me I did not know which was the key she wanted. So I gave her a handful of them and said, "Go and try these." After a while she came back smiling triumphantly and holding up the correct key. We marked it to make sure this mistake would not be repeated.

Your *willingness* to turn your life over to Christ and let Him be the Lord of it is the key to unlock the door and let Him come in to take charge. The winds of life may blow the door shut again, but always you hold the key. It belongs to you; nothing can take it from you.

If I were to tell you that you would only have to open the door once that would not be true. We use the communionware in our church many times in a year and each time we must open the door to the cabinet. When a baby is born it is not required to breathe one time only. It must continue to breathe for the remainder of its life, but it is required to breathe the *first* time before it can breathe the second.

This is what the life that is for real is all about. This is what the Christian life is all about. Learning to use the key of willingness, to be directed of God in every situation that arises in life. No one except our Lord has ever become perfect in this respect.

We will say more about using this key in our daily lives later on, but for now we are concerned with the first turn of the lock, the first breath, the beginning.

It is the first breath that leads to breathing. It is the first step that leads to walking. It is the first yielding that makes of us new persons, for we are off our own hands into God's.

Miracles start to happen when we make a beginning. We begin to discover the new nature God has given us. He has changed our likes into dislikes. He has replaced our old motives with new ones. The things we now like are the things God likes; the things we now want are the things God wants. This is only another way of saying that, in place of that old nature we discovered when we unwrapped the package, He has given us a new nature— a nature that is for real!

Now, how do I *know* this? How can I be so certain? How do I dare to stick my neck out and say it can happen to you, any time you want?

Because it has happened to me! And that is the best answer I can give. Steady a moment now . . . don't let me set myself up as a hero-figure. That would be phony.

Let me explain. When I say that Christ gave me a new nature and made me a new person, what do I mean? I mean there was a time in my life when I *enjoyed* sin (disobedience to God). I planned it ahead, I looked forward to it, and afterwards I looked back upon it with a certain sense of satisfaction and pleasure. It was fun to inflate my ego. It was fun to exploit another human being. It was great sport to open a wound in the soul of someone else as long as it was to my advantage. "Business is business," I would say.

But eventually it all turned to ashes in my mouth. And I began to experience a sense of deep dissatisfaction and uneasiness about my relationship to life and to people. The mask I wore became a heavy and brittle thing. The fleeting glimpses I had of my phoniness became more and more frequent. My relationship to my family began to sour a bit, and I began to dislike very much that person who furtively lurked behind the mask.

I found it very easy to rationalize all this and say, "Come on now, get with it! Snap out of this depressing mood!" And I would get going and run away even faster. But now God was bugging me. I began to feel more and more trapped. I fell to asking myself questions such as, "What is the *meaning* of this rat race? Why am I here? Where am I going in such a hurry? Is there anything that makes sense in the universe?" You see, I was really saying, as so many millions of frightened little people do, "How can I find God?"

Elsewhere I have told something of the climactic events that eventually began to bring me back to reality.* But the time really came when I *had* to admit I needed help. And I made a beginning. I turned my life over to the Lordship of Jesus Christ. I took the key of willingness which was mine and unlocked the door. Then the miracles began to happen. I was astounded when I began to look over the new nature God had given me. Things were topsy-turvy; they were upside down, deep down where life mattered most everything was different. My previous likes became my dislikes; my deepest motives were changed completely.

Don't misunderstand me; *my performance* did not become perfect, but my motives became purified. I still act wrongly, I still do not obey God perfectly, but there's a difference. Christ made that difference. I no longer *plan ahead* to commit sin, I no longer *enjoy* it if I slip, and I

---

*Arnold Prater, *You Can Have Joy!* (Grand Rapids: Zondervan Publishing House, 1964).

look back upon it with sorrow and remorse. It is no longer *fun* to inflate my ego or to exploit another human being. I know now that any time I open a tiny cut in the soul of another I tear a gaping wound in my own. I *want* the things God wants; I *like* the things God likes. As the old preacher said, "I ain't yet the man I want to be, I ain't yet the man God wants me to be, but thank God, I ain't the man I used to be!"

I began to breathe once; I still must breathe every day. I unlocked the door once with the key of my willingness and the miracles happened, but I still have to go to that door every day and on some days many times. There are even days when for some reason I refuse to go to the door with the key of my willingness, but since Christ has given me a different nature, I usually find myself giving in and then wondering why I even considered refusing. The old mask hangs in the closet for days and gets a bit dusty even though I sometimes reach for it. The difference is that now I don't want it. Formerly, if I thought the occasion would be profitable for me in some way, I could hardly wait to get it on.

I am telling you all this to encourage you. I want you to know that Christ can do these things for *you*.

Now, a word of caution: When you take the key of willingness and open the door, when you take your first breath, when you relinquish your whole self to Christ, don't look for the flashing lights and the giddy "way out" sense of exultation. Don't wait for the earth to shake or the fireworks to go off inside you. It may happen in just this way. Your sense of release and happiness may be so great it will overwhelm you. But remember, God doesn't come by the numbers. He doesn't come by the route of

the buttons. It isn't a matter of "I'll do it, 1-2-3 Zoom!"
God comes as *He* will and in the manner which is best
for *you*. He may come with the lightning and the thunder
or He may come like the flower seed you planted once.
You watched and waited and wondered and questioned,
but one morning, there it was!—a tiny thing, and yet
concrete evidence of the result of your act. I do not know
how He will make himself known to you, but when you
make the beginning, He will come! That I promise. That
I know.

Your self nailed him to his pain: His Self can release
you from yours!

You need not trust *my* word for this thing. In fact, if
the evidence of what has happened in my life constituted
all that is available to you, then you'd have reason to
question, or perhaps you could find an explanation for
this change of nature in some psychological theory. But
history and this present world is simply filled with evidence that is so overwhelming no one can afford to ignore
it. Medicine always looks for mass evidence before ac-
cepting a new drug. A few isolated cases won't do for
physicians. It need not be sufficient for you. There is
plenty of evidence right in your own locality if you'd
take the time to seek for it. Evidence of how Christ can
change a person from being unreal and a fake into a person cemented to reality.

Five missionaries are slain in South America. The wife
of one takes her little daughter and goes to live among
the very savages who killed her husband to tell them of
the changing power of Christ? Why?

One night an old missionary stood in the streets of the
slums of Kobe, Japan. The raw sewage from the city ran

around his ankles and the rats scurried across the filth. A little group of sad, somber, defeated people stood about him as he closed his message telling them of the love God had for them.

"Anyone want to come to Christ tonight?" he cried. And not a person moved. Once more he called, once more, nothing. Still again he called, "Surely someone will come to Him tonight."

And a little barefooted boy stepped forward. All he had on was a kind of oriental nightshirt. His hair was matted and uncombed, his body was covered with running sores and he looked up at the preacher through sad, diseased eyes and said, "Could he use me?"

The preacher looked down at him and smiled, "Yes, son, I think he could use you." He took a cup and reached down in the gutter and got some water and baptized him. Then he said, "What's your name, son?"

"Toyohiko Kagawa," replied the boy.

Go and read the thrilling story of Japan's greatest Christian—the man E. Stanley Jones said lived nearer to Christ than any person since Saint John.

Why did this happen?

The list is endless. Go to the Bible and read of Joseph, the slave who became a king; read of the stuttering introvert named Moses who became Israel's great deliverer; read of an uneducated little shepherd boy named David who grew to be his people's mightiest king. Read of an ignorant uncouth fisherman named Peter, of a despised tax collector named Matthew, of a woman of the streets named Mary. Read of a hateful vengeful, sick little man named Paul who met Christ and went about the pagan world declaring, "I know in whom I have believed!"

Read the stories of them all. Read on in history about the imprisoned Christians who went out into the arena to be torn to bits by wild beasts or who were impaled on crosses, soaked in pitch and set afire, and listen to them singing. Read on in history about the Luthers and the Husses and the Wesleys and when you have finished ask yourself the question, why? Why were all these people changed from being phonies into the real thing? How did it happen? It happened in every case and without exception because they finally said "yes" to God. They grew tired and sick of the kind of people they were, and they gave in to God and let Him make them into the kind of persons He wanted them to be. They discovered the deepest law of the universe, that "whoever would save his life shall lose it and whoever loses his life for my sake shall find it."

When you bow down and give up, phoniness begins to end, and God comes.

I should like very much to go to Copenhagen, Denmark, some day and visit the Church of Our Lady there. Ravaged by war and storm many times through the years it has stood, it was again damaged severely during the First World War. The king ordered it rebuilt, and, among other things, he commissioned the great Danish sculptor Thorwaldsen to do statues of Christ and the disciples.

Today the likeness of Christ stands behind the altar. You enter the quiet of the cathedral and sit down on the left and look for a moment. Then you notice a strange thing. You can see the statue of Christ, but you cannot see His face. So you think, "The lighting must be bad here, so I'll move." And you move to the other side of the nave and sit down, but it is the same. Everywhere you sit you can see the likeness of the Lord, but you cannot see His face. So then you slowly walk down the aisle to the chancel railing and in the hushed beauty of the moment, you fall on your knees and fold your hands. Then you look up—and you can see it! You can see His face! *Only when you are bowed down can you look up and see the face of the Christ!*

This is what you are ready to do. You are ready to give Him your life. You are ready to make a beginning. That in itself is a miracle. That in itself is a long way from phoniness.

Begin now.

# Chapter 5

## WHAT'S FOR REAL?

To believe and to fail to do is like warming one's hands at the flames of his neighbor's house while it is burning.

We have been seeking to be new persons, to be released from the necessity of being phony. It was a long bitter struggle to come to the point of surrender. But at the end of the road we found Christ waiting for us. Now He has done for us what we could never do for ourselves. His Holy Spirit has brought us all the way from rebellion to the points of admission of failure, the honest confrontation of ourselves, and finally to that greatest of all the experiences of life—of turning everything over to him.

We have made a beginning in the new life. But now it is time to go on down the road. Until now we have been dealing with our own inner attitudes; now we must deal with our outer behavior.

Here is where a lot of people want to stop. They want to stay up among the clouds of victory. They want to smell the fragrance of the heavenly places. When the emotional tonic begins to subside they feel "let down" and begin to seek feeling again. So they run from meeting to meeting seeking feeling for feeling's sake. I would be the last to decry feeling. In religion we sometimes become so impressed with ourselves and so sophisticated that we suppress all feeling and thus rob ourselves of the joy there should be between the lover and the beloved.

"My meat is to *do* the will of him who sent me," declared Jesus. So this is our next task. To take the first, tiny, infant-like step. And it deals with our behavior. We have found God; we have begun to be real, honest persons, so now we must seek to do what we believe to be His will for us.

If you will read the fourth chapter of the Gospel of John you will find a thrilling story there of Jesus and a loose-living woman whom he met at Jacob's well. When she made the marvelous discovery that even though Jesus knew every most intimate detail of her wicked life He still loved her and wanted to give her eternal life, she really got excited. She got so excited she forgot her water jar and ran to the village to tell her friends about this miracle. Her first impulse after making this marvelous discovery was to do something about it.

You have opened the beautiful package of the self you imagined yourself to be, and inside you found something from which you recoiled in horror. But when you offered that awful thing to the Lord, He took it and loved you anyhow.

Now, if there is any kind of decency in us at all, we surely will be prompted to do something about it. First we will want to begin to make right all the wrongs we possibly can—all the things that have resulted from the self we used to be, the things which spewed out into the world and damaged others—these are the things we want to make right. God has done his part and now we want to do ours. Had you noticed that miracle? I said, we find we *want* to do our part? Isn't this new? Isn't this different? Can we ever remember being motivated to right all the wrongs in our lives? And now we want to do this! These are new likes and dislikes we are discovering in ourselves. These are new motives which have begun to pop up here and there.

One of the most difficult things any human being ever has to do is to say, "I'm sorry, forgive me." We would rather say anything than that, for when we say that it robs us of our pride. To confess we have been wrong is agony to the proud spirit, but if we want to be for real, this is one of the first things God wants us to do. If we fail to do it, it will remain as a great obstacle to our growth.

There is plenty of scriptural evidence for this. First we confess our sins to God. We have done that. Listen to the ringing clarity with which this Scripture describes our experience.

> When I kept silence (before I confessed), my bones wasted away through my groaning all the day long.
> For day and night Your hand (of displeasure) was heavy upon me; my moisture was turned into the drought of summer. Selah (pause, and calmly think of that)!
> I acknowledged my sin to You, and my iniquity I did not hide. I said, I will confess my transgressions to the Lord (continually unfolding the past till all is told), then You (instantly) forgave me the guilt and iniquity of my sin. Selah (pause, and calmly think of that)!
> Psalm 32:3-5 (The Amplified Bible)

Though we are not told, I am sure in my own mind that not only confession to God but confession to one another took place between the disciples in that upper room before they received the Holy Spirit. The Bible says they "tarried" there for six weeks and that they were of "one accord," that is, they were of one mind. My guess is that it took much discussion and prayer before they reached that accord. I am sure they must have confessed their own sins to one another, for the guilt of them was fresh and hard in their minds.

In my mind's eye I can see James or John stand up and say, "I was covetous. I was greedy. I was in this thing for what I could get out of it. And the very last week of His life, I was demanding the best seat in the kingdom. I wanted to be at the top of the ladder in God's court."

There they were together. Tragedy had torn a gaping hole in their expectations. They were in the mood to ask, "What part did I play in this calamity?"

I can see Thomas summoning the courage to get to his feet, "I doubted him," he says, with sadness. "He very plainly told us that after three days He would rise again, but even after the rest of you had seen Him with your own eyes, I had to have more proof. I had to have something on which to place my hands. I could not receive your testimony by faith. I doubted Him."

Last of all, perhaps because his sins were greater and his pride deeper, Simon Peter arises. "But none of you hurt Him as badly as did I," he says. "I constantly misunderstood Him. I constantly twisted what He said into what I wanted it to mean. And finally I denied Him. In order to save my own neck I lied and said I had never heard of Him. I did it three times. And then when He needed me most, I ran away!"

I am convinced that only after they had confessed, completely cleaned house with one another, and given themselves again to God, did the Holy Spirit come.

This is precisely what we are ready to do now. I do not mean we are going to take a list of our past wrongs and run up and down the street waving them for everyone to see. I mean we are quietly going to approach those whom we have wronged and hurt. We are going to confess our part of the trouble and tell them we hope they will forgive us.

The world is full of people who profess to believe, but not very many are big enough to swallow pride, to let it melt down before God and attempt to right some of the wrongs of their past.

I remember seeing a very funny old-time movie. Of course at the end the cops were chasing the bad guys. The bad guys were in an old dilapidated Model-T. As they drove along parts started dropping off. First the top blew off, then the fenders, one at a time, then the doors and finally the body itself fell away and they were left riding on only the frame. It was terribly funny at the time. Parts of that car were strewn for miles.

In just this way, back down the roads of our lives we too have left wreckage. We want to clean it up before we go on.

So once more take paper and pencil, and let's make our list. Maybe you remember the old story of the woman who had been bitten by a mad dog. Although she was taking the proper treatment, her doctor, trying to impress her with the seriousness of the situation, said, "It's possible that you might die of hydrophobia, so you had better draw up a will!"

The woman took some paper and a pen and wrote for several minutes until finally the doctor interrupted her and said, "That's a rather lengthy will you're writing."

And the woman replied, "Oh, this isn't a will. I'm just making a list of the people I'm going to bite!"

Well, we are going to make a list of the people we have already bitten! In order to make this list we must ask ourselves some questions. We can go back to the list we made when we opened the package for some valuable clues. That old self we used to be will speak volumes to us about what we need to do to make things right.

Probably you should begin with your family—those who are the very dearest to you. They are the very ones on whom the old self used to spew out its pain. How have you been seen by your wife or husband or children? Stingy, demanding, irritable, jealous, nagging, constantly critical, neglectful, autocratic, loud talking? Just what have they seen in you that the public never saw? Other things will suggest themselves to you.

Now, your relatives. More deep resentment and bitterness exists among relatives than the world ever knows about. Some little fleabite of an incident took place years ago, and, all this time, resentment, bitterness, and even hatred has been festering in the subconscious mind, taking its toll. If needed, make a list of these hurts. Do not lose courage, there are some joyful surprises awaiting.

Out in Idaho, the government built some huge potato bins some years ago. They bought up many millions of pounds of potatoes and stored them in those bins. The bins were made of concrete, reinforced with steel and were six inches thick. But officials had not reckoned with one thing. The next spring when the sunlight struck the concrete bins its warmth was transmitted into the darkness of the interior: the potatoes began to sprout and grow. The result was that within a few short weeks every last one of the bins cracked wide open and the concrete walls were torn asunder. The power of the potatoes in the darkness when combined with the warmth of the sun could not be denied.

It is just that way with all these old resentments and guilts which have rested there on the floors of our subconscious minds. We have thought they were dormant, and some of them we thought were forgotten. But they were not dormant; they were festering and growing and swelling. One day they surged up to the conscious level and manifested themselves in physical illness or in some lashing out at others, for our internal conflicts always externalize themselves, and, sadly enough, many times on those we love the most, who are defenseless, puzzled and hurt. This is why we *must* bring them up into the light of God's will. There they shrivel and die and are melted away.

You see, you have turned your life over to God. You have named Christ as the ruler of your life. You were a phony and you sickened of it and you had to admit your sickness. So with a strange mixture of despair and hope and just a tiny bit of faith, you made a beginning. You wanted Him to be the Master of your life.

So now the question must always be, "Lord, what do *you* want me to do?" If we have not made the obeying of His will our greatest desire, then we can go right on holding grudges, nurturing bad tempers, holding to our prejudices, criticizing, hating and take the consequences.

But if we have become willing to let Him run the

whole show, then concerning those in our family whom we have crushed and hurt we are going to have to say, "Lord, what do you want me to do about this situation?" If there are relatives against whom we hold ancient resentments we are going to have to say, "Lord, what would you have me do here at this point?"

Now we must expand our list to include those in our circle of friends, those in our business lives, those in our church, and those who are back there somewhere along the roads of the past.

In most every case you will discover that the hurt you have done to another has not been as great as the hurt you have done to yourself. And now for one of the pleasant surprises: You are going to find, almost without exception, that every one whom you approach will receive you graciously. It is a rare thing in this world today to have someone come to you and ask your forgiveness. This so startles and gratifies people that many times they are overwhelmed. They *will* forgive you. But even if you meet with a rare rebuff, this will not affect in the least the sense of pure relief which you will find welling up within you. The happiest times in our lives are always the times when our will turns out to be identical with God's. The reverse of this is true also.

Of course you will need to exercise some common sense. If what you are going to do will in some way hurt another person, then forget it. You are not to cause someone else to bleed so that you can be healed. Let's set up a theoretical situation and use a very gross and crude sin as our example. Suppose you have had an affair with another man's wife or husband. It's all over now but the third party never found out about it, never suspected. Of course there would be no point in opening pain in the heart of the innocent party. To do so would be callous and would be an attempt to heal yourself at the expense of another. You might, if the opportunity arises, want to ask forgiveness of the one whom you exploited. You will be able to use good judgment as to when to speak and when to keep silent. But be careful that you do not use this as an excuse to evade the issue.

We have straightened out our relationship with God and now we are straightening out our relationship with our brother men. Our relationship with God can never be fully right until our relationships with one another are right. God has forgiven us. He has taken that twisted ugly self of ours and covered it with his Cross, his grace and his love. And now we are responding by seeking forgiveness from our fellow creatures.

You said you wanted to be a real person, you wanted to be different, you wanted release from the phony. Well, isn't this different, and isn't it new for you, and isn't it real? It certainly isn't like the old you.

Project this out onto the entire world for just a wistful moment. Suppose that on this day *every human* in the world were engaged in doing just what you are doing. Suppose that everywhere people, having been accepted and forgiven by God, were busy at the task of making things right between themselves and their brothers? What a different set of headlines you'd be reading next week! What different newscasts you'd be hearing and seeing! What a different atmosphere would surround your community, your business, your home! This is a part of what we mean when we pray. "Thy Kingdom come."

Well, which is real and which is phony? The cynic will sneer and say, "The headlines are the reality. It is mystical, dreamy-eyed people like you who are the escapists. This is a jungle of a world where the strong survive and the weak perish. Those are the brutal facts of life."

Maybe the old you said that.

But which is reality? Unreality is that which appears to be real but doesn't last, nor jibe with truth.

What is the ultimate reality about matter, for example? You see an oak tree and you walk up to it and slam your fist into it. You'd probably say, "Man, the matter which composes that tree is real—just look at my hand." And I would have to admit that it seems that the ultimate reality is matter. But this is the reasoning of a phony.

For you and I know that the ultimate reality about that tree is not physical at all. We can cut a sliver from it and take it to the laboratory and analyze its basic structure and when we do this we find that the tree is composed of cells. Those cells are composed of molecules and those molecules are composed of atoms. Those atoms are composed of infinitesimally small electromagnetic parts called electrons, protons and neutrons. These are composed of tiny bits of energy. And energy is a nonmaterial thing. It is of the essence of God. It is a part of his power. It is the stuff which He poured into the atoms. Then He used the atoms as basic building blocks for the universe, and *everything* is built using them. So the ultimate reality in the creation is not matter, even though it seems to be, and even though the majority of people live and act as if it were. What it boils down to is that if you want to be for real, you have to live in contact with that which is real.

If you want to live risking everything on that which only seems real, then you'll have to live a phony life.

Now if the ultimate reality is spiritual and not physical, which is the most real, the hatred that destroys men or love that saves them? Which is the most real, tying on to Someone who promises eternal life, or tying on to the self which promises only ultimate destruction? You don't have to be a brain to answer that one.

We would not say that the morbid headlines we read are unreal in the sense that they are not happening. We do not deny that evil exists, or that evil events occur. This is nonsense; no meaning can be assigned to such a statement.

If I am outdoors and a cloudburst comes, it would be pretty stupid of me to stand in it declaring, "This cloudburst exists only in my mind; it is not happening." It would be pretty foolish to stand out in the cold, driving rain and risk pneumonia, all the while denying that it was raining. The intelligent thing is to recognize the happening and go quickly into the house where there is warmth and protection, love and laughter.

We do not deny that there is such a thing as evil. Too m: ny happenings prove otherwise. Calvary, for example. But we do deny that the life of phoniness which seems so right to so many is real. We know now that all its bright promises of security and happiness are blatant lies and that it only leads ultimately to destruction. And that which is destroyed is no longer in contact with ultimate truth and cannot be worthwhile.

Now let's reduce the complex to the simple. Here you are, a human being, and you have made contact with the ultimate reality which is God. You have tied on to

Christ, for better, for worse, for richer for poorer, in sickness and in health. You are risking everything on the proposition that God, not evil, will have the last word. Besides, you have tried that other way and you know full well what it did to you.

So the simple fact is, God has said that his forgiveness is based on your willingness to seek forgiveness from those against whom you have trespassed, and to forgive those who have trespassed against you.

That is why you are willing to tackle this thing head on. Even if it costs you plenty in personal pride, no matter what it costs you are going to do it and do a complete job of it. But don't go about it with set, grim lips as a little boy bows his head and accepts the fact that his mother is about to scrub the back of his neck. Go about it with the quiet resolve to do your Lord's will, believing with your very best mind and heart, that this willingness to set things right is in full and complete accord with Him who is the Ultimate Reality.

When you are ready to start out making your contacts, or when you are set to make that long distance call to someone you've wrecked, or when you sit down to write that letter, you can leave off your mask! This is one time you won't be needing it. People are not going to be looking into the eyes of a phony. You are beginning to be a real person.

How new and different it is for you to be willing to suffer a bit for the sake of those who have hurt you and whom you have hurt! I have been waiting all these pages to call to your attention these wonderful words. I can wait no longer, The time is now.

> Therefore if any person is (ingrafted) in Christ, the
> Messiah, he is (a new creature altogether), a new crea-
> tion; the old (previous moral and spiritual condition) has
> passed away. Behold, the fresh and new has come!
> 2 Corinthians 5:15 (The Amplified Bible)

The fresh and new has come. The old was phony. The
old was unreal. Now the fresh and new has come! And
with your key you have become willing to let pride hurt
for the sake of others.

I want to tell you the story of a girl we'll call Hulda.
She was a little blonde, blue-eyed Swedish girl who was
a nurse in a state mental hospital in the West. She was
for real and by now you will know what that means.
Hulda was very devout and never missed a service of
worship. Oftentimes she would drop in the prayer chapel
of her church during the noon hour to spend a few moments in quiet thoughtfulness and prayer. One Sunday
morning as she sat in worship her pastor was shocked to
notice that her face was all cut, bruised and scratched.
He supposed she had, unknown to him, been involved in
an accident. When she went out the door that morning
and shook hands with him he noticed her hands were
covered with scratches and red marks. Not wishing to
pry, since she offered no explanation, he did not mention
her condition.

The last person out of the building that day was the
head nurse of the section in which Hulda worked. "What
on earth happened to Hulda?" he asked.

Then the head nurse told him. Two weeks previously
a little fourteen year old girl had been brought into the
hospital, violently insane. A day or so later the physician

in charge of that section told her story at the daily staff
meeting. The little girl had been reared in abject poverty.
Her father and mother were both alcoholics. Never in
her entire life she heard a single word of love. Never
had she been made to feel wanted and needed. Never
had she known what kindness and affection were. One
day at the age of twelve she had watched as her drunken
mother and father, in a violent argument, struggled for
possession of a shotgun. She had seen the gun fire and
watched as the life of her father ended on the floor. The
mother was charged with manslaughter and paroled,
presumably to care for the child. But in the next two
years the same old life continued and all she knew from
her mother were curses and beatings. Finally her little
mind became so filled with hatred and resentment
towards all human beings it rejected reality and snapped.
She drifted off into fantasy and delusion and became violently insane.

The physician then told the staff that a part of her
therapy must be catharsis. She must be allowed to vent
her wrath on someone, to spew out some of the pent-up
hatred which had poisoned her so. The physician then
called for volunteers. Hulda raised her hand.

Then for one hour a day for two weeks Hulda went
into the cell with this demented girl and allowed her to
have her catharsis. She took all of her kicks, all of her
pounding, all of her clawing and scratching until the
girl's strength was spent and she crouched in a corner,
trembling like a frightened, trapped little animal. Then,
as Hulda left the cell, each day she would pause at the
door, turn and face the girl. And there with her own
blood streaming down her face she would smile at the

girl and repeat these words, "Darling—I love you! Darling—I love you!"

This is like Christ. You are ingrafted in Christ. Fresh and new. What you are about to do for the sake of others is for real!

## Chapter 6

## PUT ON YOUR SKIN!

Our need to be involved in the despair of others has never disappeared. We have only tried to vaporize it with the laser beams of our own human rationalization.

In our quest for reality up until now we have dealt mostly with the negatives in our lives. Now we are going to deal with the positives. The phony life is not much concerned with other people except for the sake of their exploitation. The real life is concerned with them for the sake of their salvation, in this life and in the life to come.

You have looked up the persons whom you have wronged and have done everything possible to make things right with them. Now you are ready to launch out in the new life by looking for needs in other people. "Why this? I am not a do-gooder," you may say. No one is asking you to become a do-gooder in the sense in which that term is so often contemptuously used. That is, God does not want you to be a do-gooder in order to try and make atonement for your own sins or so that you can rub salve on your own burning conscience. This is but an extension of the phony life you have left.

You are going to become involved in the despair of

others because you recognize what we have said before, that the deepest law which is woven into the fabric of the universe is this, "Whoever would save his life shall lose it and whoever loses his life for my sake, shall find it." Jesus not only stated this law but He lived it out, and it came to its great climax at Calvary and at the tomb of Joseph of Arimathea.

Besides, you have a new motive now. You no longer see people as persons to be used, you see them as persons who are living in the same old life you had. You know that behind that slick facade they are trying desperately to show to the world there lurks in them the same sense of meaninglessness and lostness that lived within you. They are as sick of that life as you were. If there is anything you can do to help them, you are anxious to do it. Don't become frightened or skeptical now; some more joyous surprises lie ahead for you.

Turn to the tenth chapter of the Gospel of Luke. Read again Jesus' incomparable Parable of the Good Samaritan. It is a startling and vivid description of the contrast between the life which is phony and the life which is for real. Here lies a man by the side of life's road. He is wounded and helpless. He has come to the place where he cannot help himself; he is at the end of his rope. If he is not helped, he will surely die.

So along comes the priest. Since I am a minister this chills me, because this priest is as phony as a bouquet of plastic flowers. But Jesus is not picking at the priesthood, or the ministry. The priest represents the "religious type." They have the forms of religion without the godliness. They know all the right answers but never do anything about them. Before we look at him with contempt maybe we had better ask, "How many of life's wounded have *I* passed by?"

Perhaps the priest had an important meeting to attend. He might have been chairman of some committee. Maybe his appointment book was simply crammed with vital dates. At any rate, he rationalized the situation and said, "This is a busy road, there will be others along soon. They will surely help him." I do not know of a more certain sign of phoniness than this. Someone else will do the job that needs to be done.

Then along came the Levite. He was a phony, too. Jesus made that very clear. "Likewise"—just as the priest had done, he passed by his stricken brother. He just couldn't be bothered. The government would take care of this. There are social agencies for needs like this. Other people, better qualified, will see to it.

Whatever it was that happened in the minds of these two phonies, it ended up being rationalization.

Then along came the Samaritan. No doubt he was just as busy as the others. But when he sized up the situation it looked very simple to him. Here was a brother who needed him. He would help. The Samaritan (who belonged to an entirely different "denomination") was for real.

You see, there are just two types of persons in the world, the takers and the givers. Hitler, Mussolini, Stalin, Castro—they are types of the takers. Their philosophy is that it is the law of tooth and fang which prevails. The strong survive and the weak perish. "What's in it for me?" is the slide rule by which they measure every situation and every person they meet. The givers are the Schweitzers, the Livingstons, the Ghandis and our Lord

Jesus Christ. "What is the need of my brother?" This is the question that motivated them. Every community, including yours, is filled with little Hitlers, Mussolinis, Stalins, and Castros. They vary in their cleverness to disguise their true selves, but they are there and they wear the mask. They are phony. Similarly, every community has its own Schweitzers, its Livingstons and Ghandis. They have no need for the mask, they are tied on to reality. They are saving their lives because they are losing them for the sake of Him who rescued *them*.

To say it another way, God has given you something precious. He has given you a new life. He has laid his hands on your blind eyes and the scales have fallen away. You *see* things, perhaps for the first time ever. But now, the only way to possess the gift is to give it away. That is the inexorable way in which this law operates.

All about us is human need—physical and spiritual need. Out there in the hot, dusty arena of life where the battle is being staged there is a deep and mighty struggle going on within each person. No matter how they may *appear,* (you already know how phony appearances can be) they are fearful, anxious and deeply unhappy. They need help. It was Emerson who said in one of his essays, "Be kind, every man you meet is fighting a battle." You had better believe it.

There is a song "No Man Is An Island." There is a sense in which this is true, but there is also a sense in which *every* man is an island. Every man feels alone, and no matter how close our friends or our family, they never quite reach over to where we really are. Believe this about your brother and the human race begins to take on a different look to you.

There is a story about a little boy who was afraid of the dark, and each night his mother would try to reason with him, but it didn't seem to help. So one night, she was sitting on his bed and he was clinging to her, not wanting her to leave him, and she said to him, "Son, for the life of me I cannot understand why you're afraid. You're not alone. Don't you know God is with you?"

"Yes, I know that," he said, "but Mother, I want someone with skin on!" So it is with these lonely, fearful people with whom you rub shoulders every day. They need to find God, but they also need someone with skin on. Besides, many times, this is the only way God can help us, by sending someone with skin on.

Involvement. In the last chapter I quoted that great verse, II Corinthians 5:17, the verse which said that if any man is in Christ he is a new creation, which said the fresh and new has come. Now we need to look at the very next verse:

> But all things are from God, who through Jesus Christ reconciled us to Himself (received us into favor, brought us into harmony with Himself) and gave to us the ministry of reconciliation—that by word and deed we might aim to bring others into harmony with Him.
>
> II Cor. 5:18 (The Amplified Bible)

He gave to us the ministry of being someone with skins on for our brothers.

Well, just *what* precisely does this mean? Does this mean we print a sign saying, "I am a Christian, I will help you?" Do we hang this sign about our necks and stand on street corners? Does this mean we rush up to the next fellow we meet and push him back in a corner and say, "Look, bud, I know you need help and I am the guy who can give it to you?" Of course not. It means simply that we begin *now* to keep our eyes and ears open. We have a new set of spiritual ears and a new set of spiritual eyes. We use them. With our ears we can hear their cries of inner pain, whereas before, we were deaf. Now we are perceptive and can see their movements of distress whereas before we saw nothing at all except the shallow life we shared with them. Now we are *aware,* that is the best word I know for it.

When you drop the mask and begin to edge away from phoniness, do you renounce the "old crowd"? That is, do you just cancel out all your friends of the former phony life and seek out a group that sees things as you do? No, *they* are the very people you may have a chance to help. You *know* how they need help. Nobody need spell that out for you.

In the beginning, the only thing that has changed is *you.* You don't go and preach to them. It is what you *are* that will open the door for you and for God, with them. I think one of the greatest book titles of this century is *Love Is Something You Do!** Love is not just what you say, it is what you do.

You just begin to move in among your friends with the mask off. You don't *have* to impress them any longer, you have been liberated from your need for the phony. You are simply quietly confident that you are God's child, that's all. No speeches, no sermons, no grandiose finger pointing. You just move quietly among them in the confidence that you are God's and he is yours. You see, our

---

*Frederick B. Speakman, *Love Is Something You Do!* (Westwood, N. J.: Revell, 1959).

natural inclination is to want to do too much too quickly. But you have ripped off your mask before God and let his light shine on you in honesty, and that honesty is bound to be reflected. Some of them will see it, and in God's own good time, one by one, your friends will open the door for you to tell them what has happened to you.

But you must *listen* for their cries of pain. You must listen for their cries for help. Very likely, they will not come bursting into your office someday and say, "I need help, and I've noticed lately that you seem to have something different. I want what you've got!" This is not very likely to happen. What will happen is that they will throw out a feeler. If you miss the boat, they will retreat. Let me give you a couple of examples.

One day a man came into the outer part of my office. He walked straight over to the church secretary and said he wanted to know the state of his pledge to the church. How much he had given so far this year? The door to my office was open and I called out a greeting to him. He came and stood in the doorway and we chatted for a few minutes. Then he edged into the office. I invited him to sit down. I stopped talking and let him take over. Before long he ran out of pass-the-time-of-day talk. Then he leaned forward and said, "I've got to talk to you about something serious in my life." From there on he poured out his problem. But suppose I had not called out to him? Many people come to the office of the church to inquire about their giving. They have no other reason for coming. But they *might!* And that's the point of the whole thing. Listen for their cries.

One morning the phone rang at the wrong time (does it ever ring at the right time?) I was hours behind the schedule I had laid out that day. In spite of myself, I felt tension begin to build up. There were some things I *had* to do. There was an important appointment I simply could not afford to miss. The irritation mounted up within as I lifted the receiver. It was a woman who wanted the address of someone in the church who had moved away. Now she could very easily have obtained that from the church secretary. Ah, here was the clue. In spite of my high blood pressure mood God rang the warning bell in my mind. So I gave her the address and then said, "How've you been lately?" That's all it took. Gradually she began to tell the real reason she had called. I won't go into detail, but suffice it to say that what happened in her life that day was far more important than anything which I had planned for my day.

Suppose I hadn't heard the bell? Listen for their cries. As I was writing this chapter in a motel I said to the cleaning woman, "My, you're a busy worker." She straightened up and replied, "I've got to keep busy."

The bell rang. It turned out that six months previously her husband of forty years had died of cancer, after a long, lingering illness. She needed to talk about it. She needed desperately to find someone who would just listen. It was killing her to keep it all choked up within. Listen for their cries.

If you are original, many creative ways will suggest themselves to you, and the Holy Spirit will help.

You sickened of the old phony life, you became bored stiff with its meaninglessness and its constant demands for the mask. So you found the way to Christ. You opened the package and gave what was inside to Him forever. In return He gave you a new self, a maskless self: He tied you on to reality. Now to *you* He has given a small part of this ministry of reconciliation, of helping to bring others into harmony with Him.

Some people who are for real deliberately seek to make their own opportunities. I know a man who is vice-president of a great corporation in this country. Once a week he calls one of his friends or business associates to make a luncheon date. His key of willingness is constantly turning the lock in the door. He is listening for the cries of his brothers. He makes it a point to give his luncheon companion an opportunity to talk about life on his island. He does not press the issue, just leaves the door slightly ajar. Many times, he tells me, people will rush through that door. Others will come through it very slowly. Still others will ignore it and not come through at all. But he stays on the job.

Once a month he and his wife invite to their home from among their wide circle of acquaintances some couples in whom they have seen a sign of distress. They spend the evening together and at sometime during the evening he drops a remark which is an invitation to them to "open up." Here the experience is the same: many rush in eagerly, others hesitantly, and others not at all.

Involvement in the despair of others—this is the essence of love. Perhaps your circle of friends is too small. It may need to be enlarged. You may need to become more active in some service organization—anything to broaden the scope of opportunities God can seize.

And above all things you need the church. Now here some may shy away. But at this point I am adamant. There is no doubt the church is under attack today and with some justification. But you need it in your life, if for no other reason than the fact that the Church is of God. It is His: He bought it with His own sacrifice and He has nurtured and maintained it through the ages in spite of its imperfections. The fact still remains that it is the only organization in the world in which the admission that you are unworthy is a requirement for membership. You need it too for the value of public worship. God is able to do things corporately which he cannot do privately. You are going to see much that is phony in the church. And that is because it is composed of people. You will run smack dab into ecclesiastical laryngitis, numerical neurosis, and numbing trivia. But don't let this frighten you away from the feast.

Not too long ago I had the privilege of going down to south Missouri to preach in a little rural church. Following the service there was "dinner on the ground"—a real old-fashioned "basket dinner" where each family brought enough food for themselves and more and spread it together out on the church lawn on a common table. Anything I could say about the abundance of foods of all kind, the aroma, the delightful variety, would be gross understatement. But there were also a few foods on that bountiful table which I did not like. I thoroughly detested them. Someone had brought some summer squash, someone else some baked parsnips, someone else some sour cherries. For all I know these may be your favorite foods, but they are at the bottom of my list. What if I had said, "Well, I'm not going to partake of this food. There are a few things here I don't like so I will just by-pass this golden-brown fried chicken, this home-cured country ham, these scalloped potatoes, and all those delicious pies and cakes. Just count me out." If I had announced that, someone would surely have called for the doctor. I assure you I made no such statement, but simply bypassed the foods which were unpalatable to me and fed my body.

This is needful for you. Christ is the Lord of the church; it is His. He does not love it because it is perfect, He loves it because it is His. Christ is your Lord, too. This you have acknowledged with all your heart. He does not love *you* because you are perfect, He loves you because you are His.

His Spirit is not limited to the church but it works there and has for two thousand years. He sustained it through all the twisted, perverted concepts of the Middle Ages when men used it as a vehicle with which to exploit their brothers. Now that the jet age has come and many are raising the cry of "irrelevant" it is doubtful to me that God has suddenly decided last week to abandon his church!

If there are phonies in the church, then they will need you. You will need to cultivate them. They are the hardest kind to win, but they need the most help.

You have accepted Jesus Christ as your Lord, go and do as he commanded, be baptized and join His church so that you might stand up and be counted as one of His.

Perhaps you are already a member of His church, but you have been a phony and you know it. Now that you have come this far back from the far country, go to your pastor and say to him, "I want to make a rededication of my life. I haven't been the kind of a member of Christ's church I promised I'd be. But I want to begin again!" You will be amazed at the joybells that will begin to ring in your heart and in his!

But you'll find something else in every church if you will only look for it. You will find a group of people—it may be small—to whom Christ is everything. And from them you will gain much of the strength and encouragement you need. No one who tries to go it alone ever gets very far spiritually.

A good many people compartmentalize the church because they see it only as an institution. If, they feel, they are not serving in the organizational structure of the institution, they are not serving the church. Nothing could be further from the truth.

The fact is that every person is the church. Now I know this is not a new statement by any means, yet many fail to grasp it. When you leave the worship service on Sunday and go into Monday you become the very church at every point, in each and every instance where your life touches the life of another person. For there is only one place you can practice the religion of Jesus Christ, and that is at the point where your life touches another. Here you are either phony or real. Here you either fake it or are genuine.

You cannot practice the religion of Christ upon a brass cross or a stained glass window or upon some great and magnificent pulpit. You worship God in the presence of these things, but only when you become someone with skin on at the point where your life touches another does your faith become meaningful.

So now in this exciting business of living in reality you see people in a new and different light. When you were opening the package of the self you asked yourself, "What do I do to other people?" Now you constantly ask yourself, "What does God want me to do *for* this person?" What a different you! Now your eyes are wide open, you are learning to look behind the mask others wear, you are *aware* of the great pools of need lying deep in each life. You are constantly listening for their cries for help.

Jesus came and lived among us for thirty-three years. He looked over the human dilemma and sized us up thoroughly. Then he said, "You only need one thing, only one new commandment—love one another! That's what you need!"

Your rescue is by grace—God's grace—and not by your good works. You are not laying up credit on the black side of the ledger. You simply have a new set of motives which make you want to be a doer of the word and not a hearer only.

Some time ago I was visiting in the hospital and had started down the hall towards the front door when suddenly I was frozen in my tracks by a piercing scream, "Somebody—Somebody—help me! Help me!" Obviously it came from someone who was delirious, but as I went outside it came to me that out there in the world, out there in the midst of all that hatred, guilt, fear, despair and well-masked anxiey, there is arising a great corporate cry from a desperate humanity: "Somebody—Somebody —help us! help us!"

You and I know who the Somebody is that can help them. You and I know just Who it is that can save them from their phony lives, from their excruciating boredom, from their search to find sense and meaning. His name is Jesus the Christ. He has done it for us. He can do it for them.

Get involved with them in their despair. Listen for

their cries. Then tell them in an honest way just exactly what your experience has been. Tell them what God can do for them, too. How these fellow creatures of ours are longing to find persons who care about them!

The machinery of our modern lives is a fearsome and wondrous thing. Life whirls along at a furious pace and everyone is caught up in it. It runs so fast and furious that many are toppling out of it unnoticed and unobserved.

Some time ago I read a tragic story in the newspaper. A little five year old boy was playing in a deep ditch where a water main was being laid. He caught his foot between the pipe and the side of the ditch and could not free himself. A huge earth-moving machine was coming along, pushing the dirt back into the ditch, covering the pipe. The boy screamed and waved and shouted. He did everything he could to attract the driver's attention. But the driver could not hear him; the noise of the machine was too loud, and he covered the little lad with earth, taking his life.

From behind the masks of untold thousands today are coming the cries of people rapidly approaching the point of desperation. But many of their cries go unheard. The noise of the self-oriented machinery of our culture is drowning them out. And they are perishing.

How your crowd needs *you*, God's man, to be someone with skin on who will hear their cries—someone who will listen, who will have empathy, who will care.

Bishop Eugene Frank tells of visiting in Germany a camp for displaced persons—refugees from the East, separated from families. No one knows what to do about them. Not many care. There were long rows of plain, unpainted barracks with tarpaper roofs. People were crowded in them like animals in trucks going to market. The guide who was conducting this party of Christians took them into one of the barracks, and they looked around. There was a refugee woman there in dirty, worn clothing. Her face was gaunt, thin and tired. Huddled about her like little bedraggled chickens were four small children, wide-eyed and frightened. The guide told them that the woman had arrived the day before. She did not know where her husband was, she was lonely, heartsick and in a strange land. She had no idea what the future held for her and the children.

There was an American Christian woman in the touring group, and as the guide told this story the tears began to roll down her face. The refugee mother, unable to understand English, heard the guide talking about her. Suddenly the tear-filled eyes of the Christian woman locked with those of the refugee mother and in an instant they just rushed across the room and fell into one another's arms, sobbing their hearts out. This is the empathy to which language is no barrier. This is the compassion of God in Jesus Christ which He gives to His children so that they can become involved in the despair of their brothers.

This is the treasure which He has given you. It cost Him His life. It will cost you yours. But in losing your life for His sake, you will find it.

And when you find it, it will no longer be phony. It will be real.

# Chapter 7

## THE PHONY ALWAYS FADES!

An impersonal knowledge of God is like the tail feathers of a peacock—highly ornamental but not much use in a high wind.

You are tied on to reality now, but we want to make certain your faith remains firm, for you will surely be tested along the way. If you have gotten the idea that you are going to sail along on clouds of heavenly bliss the remainder of your life, forget it.

Life is not set up that way for anybody. There are going to be moods of the body and mind. And all of us, by the very nature of things, live constantly under the possibility of personal tragedy, calamity and catastrophe. The thing which we now wish to make secure and firm is our faith. If it rests on the solid rock, then *nothing* can shake us loose from it.

Why do Christians crack up? Why is it that the way is strewn with those who began the new life once but for some reason fell by the way? The roll of any church tells the sad story of those who began the more excellent way once but at some point in whose journey discouragement, indifference, or complacency took over.

Some time ago a Sunday School teacher in a northern state embezzled over $200,000 from a bank. She taught a class of nine-year-old boys.

A prominent member of a western community ran off with his secretary. This man was chairman of the board of his church.

A widow committed suicide two years after her husband's death. She left a note saying, "I cannot go on without him."

Well, why? Why do Christian people sometimes crack up? All Christian crack-ups do not make the headlines. A housewife becomes increasingly bitter and resentful about her lot. A harried mother breaks down and ends up in a sanitarium. A worker is fired because he cannot get along with his superiors. A business man quits the church in a huff. We could go on and on. Why do these things happen?

I do not propose to try and analyze these cases, but only to deal with what I deeply believe to be the root cause behind most all of it. We don't want it to happen to you. It need not happen. If the place where you stand with your faith is solid ground, it will not happen; indeed, it *cannot* happen! I promise you that.

The root cause of these failures lies in mistaken beliefs about the nature of God. If the deepest belief we have about him is false, then it will not sustain us when we need it most. And the most common mistaken belief of all is that *God is primarily a remote Creator.*

Note that word "primarily." The concept has grown in the minds of those who fail that the God of all is, before all things else, a remote Creator. It is not because they do not believe in God, it is the kind of God in which they believe that leads to their downfall. The first picture that formed in their minds as children was that of an omnipotent, all-knowing, all-seeing, far-off, heavenly Father—as the hippies sometimes say, a "big Daddy in the skies."

Well, God *is* the creator. He caused the creation. We gaze up at the stars and planets, all performing without flaw in response to the laws built into them, and we sing:

> I see the stars. I hear the rolling thunder, Thy power throughout the universe displayed.

There are days in our lives we remember as our "shining times." I remember one such occasion. I took our family out into the countryside one spring day when the dogwood was at its flowering peak. We spread our picnic supper in a peaceful valley. A hypertensive little brook rushed merrily at our feet. The trees were a lovely combination of breathtaking greens. The ancient hills were yet brown rolling sheets punctuated only by the periods and quotation marks of wild flowers. The grateful thought stabbed my mind, "Could anyone else but God have done all this? Could anyone else but God think of making a tree by beginning with atoms and molecules? Who else could take the same atoms with which He made these lovely trees and create the very rocks on which we sit, and form this happy, rushing brook? Only God—only God could have done this. I believe in God!"

Yes, people believe in God. Practically everybody believes in Him. Even though their lives don't show it, even though they are phony and unreal and are living within the great stream of dissatisfaction, still, if you ask them, they would say they believe in God. Even as they disintegrate and go to pieces, they believe in God. But it is the *kind* of God in which they believe that eventually gets them into trouble. This is the kind of belief that causes some people to say, "Well, I don't have to attend worship. I can get more from going off to some lake somewhere or some great spot of natural beauty." Of course they can because their God is in the clouds or the trees or the water. He is a remote Creator and His handiwork is beautiful to behold.

In their deepest minds the first verse of the Bible is the *foundation* for their faith. "In the beginning, God created . . . ." God is primarily a Creator. But in this they miss the boat and their faith is resting on sand. Of course He is the First Cause, the awe-inspiring designer of the planets and the atoms. But He is *not primarily* this.

Small wonder men grope about in the world seeking for something they never find. Small wonder people whose faith is constituted of this concept go to pieces when life caves in upon them. No wonder the nerves of men and women crumple like tissue paper under the stresses and strains of the dizzying life in the twentieth century. It is easy to see why people today, like Adam and Eve in the beginning, continue to believe they can live as they please and get away with it.

For the deepest belief they have about God is that He is really impersonal. He isn't really too concerned about them except at the time for the surgery or the day of the funeral. The thing which concerns Him most is providing pretty flowers and blue skies for them to enjoy. Their deepest belief about Him is that He is the Chief Holy Engineer with rocks, streams and mountains as His hobby and that He loves to spend His time making the rains and putting colors into dozing daisies. They can live life on the plane of the self, and God, the Divine Engineer, won't mind too much, for His chief interests lie elsewhere.

I conducted the funeral services for a man who built his life on this sort of concept. He was a great outdoorsman and never had time for the church or for other people. The song he wished to have sung at his funeral was, believe it or not, "Home On the Range." This is a subconscious thing with most people. This man, of course, represented the extreme, but unconsciously the great cloud of conviction settles in the minds of people that the great and almighty God is a magnificent and noble-bearded architect, seated at His drawing board and operating the machinery of His works.

This kind of thinking produces some results which are inevitable. I constantly see them in the lives of people. The first result is that no person who believes that God is chiefly concerned with His creation can believe that God is interested in him *personally* and with his ordinary, everyday routine.

The gap between the God of the planets and stars and their own desks, or cars, or kitchens is just too wide. It is impossible for a person who believes vaguely in God the Creator to believe that God cares about his business troubles, that God is genuinely interested in the way he treats his customers. He cannot really believe that God is concerned when he has a headache, or when the bills are unpaid, or the car payment due. He cannot think that God cares whether Junior goes steady at the age of 14. He could not really believe that God is companionable on a fishing trip, or on the golf course. No woman whose deepest belief is in God the Creator could possibly believe that He is available for radiant companionship during her daily routine while she sweeps and dusts or scrapes the mud from the children's boots. No student who thinks of God primarily as the masterful maker of all could ever believe that he cares about such things as exams, coke parties and football games.

So when their testing comes, as it surely comes to all, and when their dreams fall in shattered bits about their feet, these are the people who cry out with the psalmist, "O that I knew where I might find him!" Or they will say, "I was a Christian and God let me down!" Or in their moment of crisis they will declare, "I prayed but my prayers seemed to go no higher than the ceiling!"

You see? Their God is *high up*. He is off up in the hills somewhere watching a cocoon hatch out while they are shedding tears of grief. He is out on some nothern lake telling the wild geese it is time to go south while their hearts bleed with pain. He is out seeing after the lilies of the field while the reservoirs of their lives slowly fill with catastrophe and heartbreak.

He is not personalized. He is a great, gray mass of gelatinous variegation flitting from star to star and from planet to planet.

Well, if God is not first of all a far-off creator, what is he? You have left the life of phoniness, you have ripped that old mask away and turned your life over to God. What kind of God?

The New Testament makes it very clear that the kind of God revealed to us in Jesus Christ is, first of all, *a lover of his children.*

If we are parents, it should not be difficult for us to grasp this. For you are not primarily a carpenter, or a merchant, a teacher or a salesman. If you are a woman, you are not primarily a cake-baker, or a bed-maker, or a seamstress. These are the secondary things in your life. If you are a parent, you are, before all things else, a lover of your children. And this is the primary nature of God. He loves His children. Incidentally, the first thing we ought to be teaching our children is not that "God made you" but that "God loves you." He loves His children and the Bible says that His dwelling place is with men. That means us!

God was out there in that peaceful valley where I took my family. But He was not in the dogwood trees. God is not a molecule or a squirrel. God was not up in the blue sky. He is not a celestial astronaut who orbits the planets and galaxies. He was not in that rushing little brook; His *power* was in these things. It was His power which created them and set them to functioning according to laws.

The truth is that God was out there in that peaceful valley but He was *in us!* His Holy Spirit, which is only another way of saying His "Holy Presence," was in us as we sat there worshipping Him. He was with His children. He said He would be there, He said that lo, He would be with us always. He was keeping that promise. He was with His children as any good father wants to be.

God does not speak to the flowers, the birds, and the trees. They have no personal need of him. What does a flower know of love? When has a tree been stunned by tragedy? No babbling brook ever faced the hell of an overwhelming, compulsive temptation. No rocky hillside ever felt the bitter sting with which death robs.

The Spirit of God is with men. He is with *you* now. You have felt the faint stirrings. Your awareness may be such a new thing that it is tiny, but it is a fact it will grow.

God is with you. You see, before He created, He *loved,* and that is *why* He created. This fact alone ought to give us our most thrilling clue to his nature.

Now when you can come to believe that . . . then your faith is founded on something that *nothing* in this life can ever shake, no matter what. Stop and read that great, thrilling hymn of victory in the last three verses of the 8th chapter of Romans. You'll find it saying that *nothing* can separate us from the love of God.

In the life that is real you will soon come to know this glorious fact. How sad that so many of your friends who are still caught up in the phony life don't know this!

The Good News is that they *can* know. And the greatest clue of all is the picture of the Cross. At Calvary the God of all the galaxies and all the universes is shouting to us in crystal clear terms, "I care. I love you. I love you *this* much!"

But it took you and me a long time to develop the wrong and hurtful idea that God is an absentee creator. It may take some time for us to recover from it completely. Here is where the new life comes in. With the new you not only come different motives, but the need for different habits. Whereas before you rushed through the day without a thought of God, now you must—and we have to emphasize that word—you *must* spend some time with Him.

Cut out a segment of time when you can be alone with Him. A time when you can expose yourself, like a lifted

chalice, to Him to be filled, renewed, and taught. It must
be a time during the day when you are at your best.
Some people are like owls and are the sharpest at night,
just prior to retiring. Still others are like roosters and
function at their best early in the morning. You will
know yourself.

This will not be just a time of prayer. It helps to take
paper and pencil, for this is something definite. Do not
dwell on the morbid past. You have already done this
and received His complete forgiveness. Dwell only on the
immediate. Only on yesterday. You will again want to
ask yourself these questions as you go over the happenings of the day, "What did I do to other people?" "What
could I have done for other people?" "Did I miss an opportunity?" Do not dwell on just the negative. If you
had an opportunity and tried as best you knew to seize
it, thank God for it. If you muffed the ball, ask His forgiveness and accept it. Write down the things you have
learned from Him that day. Write the new thoughts that
have entered your mind, the new insights.

Then spend some time with His word. Unless you have
a commentary, it is best to begin in the New Testament.
Don't set a goal for yourself to read a definite number
of chapters, but read consecutively. God's Spirit still
speaks to us through His word. This is what we mean
when we say the Bible is the "living word." We don't
mean it is magic. But we do mean that in our quiet time
we always breathe a prayer that if He has a special message just for us we shall be led to it.

Let me give you an example of the living Word. Once
I had a real problem where an issue of right and wrong
was involved. I was torn between doing the right thing

and the wrong. Rationalization made the wrong thing seem to be plausible and even reasonable. Yet I was uneasy about it.

One morning (I seem to function best in the morning) I came to the Scriptures and asked God to speak to me through His word if that was His will for that day. I happened to be reading in Galatians that week, and I came to the verse where Paul asks himself the question, "Am I trying to win the favor of men, or of God?"

That was it! The Holy Spirit took those words, yanked them from the page and stamped them in my heart in an instant and I knew I had my answer.

Perhaps it won't be that definite with you every day: it isn't with me. But those times will come and *always* one receives insights when he approaches the Word in this manner.

Then in our quiet time, of course we listen. We always do this before we begin to speak to Him. So often we just bombard God with the incessant blasts of our needs much as if He were our private secretary taking dictation. Always listen first. He will put the thoughts you need in your mind and then you can pray.

Be sure the mask is not on. It was amazing to me when I learned that many times we put it on when we approach Him, but I have long since learned that God is never insulted as long as I am honest. He does not grow indignant if I tell Him, "Lord, you know I don't feel your nearness today. You know I don't even feel like praying. But I am not trusting in my feelings for I know how fickle they are. I am trusting in you. You know how I feel anyhow, but it liberates me to be honest with you."

Be honest always. At no point is life without a mask

any more joyful than at the point of complete honesty in prayer. Many times I have begun to pray, not feeling like it, and then ended up finding it difficult to cease praying because I enjoyed it so. Then, if it is morning, walk out into the day with Him and begin to live the life that is tied onto reality. Take Him with you all through the day. Pause many times just for a second and acknowledge His Presence, even if it is nothing more than a sentence or breathing of His name.

Some days will go better than others. There will be moods, but *no day* will ever be completely lost either to you or to God when you live like this!

How different this is from the old life of phoniness, so crammed full of entire days spent faking it, moving along in the stream of life knowing that there was no real meaning to it only insofar as one could satisfy the self. How different it is now! What a kick not to be living a lie!

So, set apart this slice of time just for Him.

Somewhere I heard the story of a man who came to his pastor. His mind was all cluttered with guilt and tension and everything else that comes from the life that is not for real. His pastor asked, "Do you believe in God?"

Of course, the fellow, who belonged to the church, was shocked that his pastor had asked him a question like this. "Why, certainly, I believe in God. Why do you ask?" he answered. But his pastor insisted, "Do you really believe God is with you?"

"Yes," answered the man, "But how can He help me?"

And the wise pastor replied, "He can't unless you let Him." Then he went on, "Let me paint a picture for you. Suppose we could search the world over and find a surgeon skillful enough to do what was needed in your case, who could cut a hole in the top of your head while you were under anesthetic, and who could take one of his instruments and go in and cut and scrape and work until he had removed every last one of these poisonous thoughts, fears, depressions, and evil tendencies which you say you have. Wouldn't that be tremendous?"

"Yes," said the man, "that would be wonderful."

"Now, I'll tell you something even more wonderful," said the pastor. "What if I were there with you in the operating room and before the surgeon sewed up the incision, I should take a bundle of all the precious promises of the Bible, especially the ones which promise that God's love is greater than our sin, that He will always be with us, and what if I should place that bundle in your head and just fill it with all those great truths? Then if the incision were closed and somehow you were able to replace all those harmful and hurtful things with the power and assurance of God's truths you could truly become a new person. Wouldn't that be great?"

"Oh," cried the man, "if only such a thing could be true."

And the minister said quietly, "It not only can be true, but it is true. The only difference is that you must take the time and trouble to let God empty your mind of these things and begin to fill it with positive and powerful thoughts—thoughts of faith and thanksgiving and forgiveness and conviction that if God is for you nothing can ever prevail against you!"

Just this is what Christ does in this new life which is real when we give him a chance at us every day. Remember the wording—we are "ingrafted" with Christ.

His mind becomes a part of ours. And elsewhere it is spoken of in this manner, "Having in you the mind which is in Christ Jesus."

It is not an easy way, this self-discipline in the new life, and if your experience proves to be like mine there is going to have to be a kind of "heavenly stubbornness" on your part to persist.

One morning when I woke up Cloud Nine, where I had been dwelling, had disappeared, but I learned that this is not really important. For gradually the insight came that sometimes nothing succeeds like failure. If you ever get to the point where you feel you have arrived, you're in trouble. The truth is that more often than not when you are convinced you are a failure, you are truly well on the way to becoming a success.

I said sometimes nothing succeeds like failure. What did I mean? Well, the Cross of Jesus Christ was the symbol of a colossal failure, at least in the eyes of those who were trying to follow him. Just a few days earlier they thought their ship had come in. When he entered Jerusalem the crowds cheered and shouted, "Hosanna, blessed is He that comes in the name of the Lord!" And if there had been a popularity contest in Jersualem, Jesus of Nazareth would have won, hands down. But now their ship had not come in, it had sunk. The very crowd which had shouted "Hosanna" had turned their cries into "Crucify Him!"

And they dragged Him off with a couple of common thieves, nailed His flesh to the wood and lifted Him up to die. Then they danced about His Cross and chanted their songs of hatred and taunted Him; they gouged Him with a spear and mocked Him with vinegar until His weary, broken heart stopped at last and He died.

There it stood—dark, bleak, desolate against the black skyline of the approaching storm—the Cross, the instrument of death, the mute symbol of the catastrophic failure of one life.

He was finished, they thought. The kingdom which they hoped He would establish decreased to the size of a grave, and they carried Him off and buried Him. He was finished, defeated. Dead. A failure, a tragic, disillusioned, pathetic failure. Just one more man who had thought He could change things in the world. He had failed.

They thought He had failed, and if I had been there, I should have thought so too. But wait a minute? Is this failure? Is it failure when sometime during those next few hours life surges forth again in the dark confines of that tomb? Is it failure when the graveclothes are neatly laid aside and the great stone which sealed the tomb is rolled away and one sits on that stone declaring to an incredulous world, "He is not here—He is risen, as He said!"

No, it was not failure. It was a failure which had "success" stamped on it beyond their wildest dreams.

And you will arise, too, when you think you have failed, because you are not tied on to something unreal. The phony fades and is done in, but the real always comes back. Never be deceived by the seeming defeats of the moment.

No tomb can hold you—ever!

# Chapter 8

## THE MASKLESS WAY!

Affirmation is the hammer with which you constantly pound the nail of faith. Finally the nail is driven into the board of life where it holds fast.

The old masquerade party is still in progress all about you; you are still in attendance by necessity. But you have taken off your mask and are moving quietly among the people. You have turned your back on the phony. The memory of that kind of life is still fresh in your mind, but the thrill of liberation that has been yours is fresher still. You never dreamed life could be like this. To be able to close your eyes at night with forgiveness and peace in your heart because you are tied on to reality has turned life upside down and wrongside out for you. You want others whom you know and love to unmask themselves too, and there is an ache within because they won't try it.

This is like the story I heard somewhere of the soap-box agitator who stood before a knot of people. His neck-tie was loosened, his clothing wrinkled, and his face filthy with dirt.

"Christianity has failed!" he shouted. "It has been

here for 2000 years, and just look at the condition of the world!"

A Christian standing nearby retorted, "Yes, and soap and water have been in the world for millions of years, and look at the condition of your face!"

Christ's way has never really been tried by the world. But you have started and that's what is important.

By now we have learned that the new way without the mask is not easy. It is hard, but so was the way up Calvary. We know that discouragements will come and that sometimes we'll feel like giving up. Right then is when we need to remember what we found in the package and to compare it with what we have found in this way which is real.

What we need to do is forget the past and go on. Paul wrote his determination to do this:

> Forgetting what lies behind and straining forward to what lies ahead, I press on towards the goal to win the (supreme and heavenly) prize to which God in Christ Jesus is calling us upward.
> Philippians 3:13-14 (The Amplified Bible)

That makes sense, psychologically and spiritually. It makes sense from the standpoint of mental health and physical well-being.

If anybody ever had a lot to forget, it was Paul. Think of what he would have become if he had dwelt on the memories of how he went roaring into the Christian worship services, breaking them up, arresting the worshippers and throwing them all into prison and sure death. He had memories of that day when he said, "Here, men, I will hold your coats while you take up stones and do this fellow Stephen in. Kill him! Get him out of the way. Death to the Christians!"

What a wreck Paul would have been had he dwelt on that. But here he is giving the new Christians at Philippi advice which he has made real in his own life, "Forgetting what lies behind . . . I press on."

Perhaps you are a teen-ager or a college student. You haven't had many years in which to become a phony, but you have done a pretty good job of it in a short time. Now you have taken off the mask and begun the life that is real. Now the Holy Spirit is saying to you through Paul, "Forget what is behind and press on!"

Or perhaps you have passed the alloted Biblical time. You are past threescore and ten, your life employment is ended, perhaps your mate is gone, and you have allowed yourself to fall into the habit of looking back. Well, God has a word for you, too. Press on. How dare you think God would let you live if there were nothing left for you? What kind of a God would say? "Now I want you to sit around and daydream and be bored." No, press on! This life of the self-pitying hermit is as phony as that of the younger who are still caught in the rushing river of no purpose.

Will you join with me at the point where we find ourselves now in moving an altar into our hearts and making some mighty affirmations? Will you say, "I will forget the past; God has forgiven me, I will forgive myself and press on. I will make these affirmations now"?

The first affirmation of faith I would invite you to make with me is this: "From here on, *my life will have a purpose!*"

So many persons live out their days with no fixed, concrete purpose, and, as a consequence, they are constantly knocked down by their dilemmas instead of being lifted up by their dreams.

It is from here on that counts. From now. "From this day forward," as we say in the marriage ceremony.

There are thousands of young people whose entire aim in life is to go to college, get married, have beautiful children, work like mad to get a lovely home in the suburbs, go on nice vacations, have two cars and give dinner parties for influential friends. There is nothing wrong with these things, but if it is only for the purpose of self-satiety, then it is phony and a mirage which promises but has no reality. If this becomes the great purpose of my life, then one day the meaninglessness of it will catch up with me, for these things dissolve and perish. Homes wear out; cars rust out; friends die and move away; children grow up, marry, and leave; and when it is all over, I must say, "It was all for me." There is no real *meaning* in the phony life—ever.

Life ultimately becomes like a handful of sand: while we stand and hold it, trying to decide what to do with it, behold! it has run out through our fingers and there is no more.

A friend of mine told me this little story. One Fourth of July, when his son was about six years old, he gave him a Roman candle, showed him how to hold it, and then lit it. Well, the little fellow had never seen a Roman candle before, and as the balls of fire began to shoot out— puff! . . . there went one—puff! . . . there went another—the little boy became frightened and started screaming, "Daddy, Daddy, what shall I do with it? What shall I do with it?" And all the while the balls of fire were shooting out—puff! . . . puff—until they were all gone, and in his hands the little boy held only the charred remains.

So untold millions of people in this hopped-up culture of ours—some in their teens, some with gray in their hair, and some with the palsied hands of the aged—stand holding life in their hands and crying figuratively, "What shall I do with it? What shall I do with it?" until life has run out for them and all that is left is the charred remains of frustration, bitterness and boredom.

When Jesus said, "Lay not up for yourselves treasures on earth," He was not saying that we should not have the nice things of life—not at all. He was saying that if the main purpose of our lives lies in treating the material as if it is the ultimate reality, then we are phony, and the rust and moths and thieves will eventually prove it to us. When He said, "Lay up for yourselves treasures in heaven," He was saying, "Tie your lives tight to reality for that will never perish"—a purpose in life that is shot through with the divine, a purpose that acknowledges "I am not only my brother's keeper; I am also my brother's *brother!*"

Now there is a second affirmation I would invite you to make with me from the altars of our hearts. "From here on, *my life will have content.*"

Phoniness has no content. It is like a puff-ball from an oak tree: it has volume, but when it is squeezed, there is nothing inside.

By content, I mean I will not seek to save myself by mere busyness—by doing only the trifling, so that I can keep busy and thus give the impression that I am contributing much to life.

How many people there are like this! They are the busiest people in the world, their calendars are full to the limit, their pace is frantic, but their lives have no content. They are phony, fake, and unreal.

Down in the Ozark hills we used to have a name that fits them. We used to call them "latherers." Do you know what a latherer is? Uncle Melvin had one. His name was Billy. He was a mule. Uncle Melvin had a sawmill and kept several teams of mules. The loggers would hitch them to the logging wagons and go out into the timber, cut down trees, trim them, and load the heavy logs on the wagons. The mules would pull the logs back to the mill. The men knew Old Billy as a latherer. He would puff, pant, and snort, and he'd become all foamed up; he'd prance and lower his head and try to make you think he was the pullingest mule ever known. But the truth was he always lagged in the harness. His mate had the main bulk of the load on his shoulders while Old Billy pranced and snorted and faked it. Old Billy never fooled the loggers. They knew a good performance when they saw it and they knew the other kind. No doubt Old Billy was exhausted at night, for there is nothing more exhausting than trying all day to pretend.

There is a big difference between doing the big things in life and living a life which has content. Most of us will never be able to do the big spectacular things. We won't paint a great canvas, or compose a symphony, or lead in science, or do any one of a number of big things. Not many of us are going to be recorded in history books. But all our lives can have content. That's what we've been trying to say since page one.

By content, I mean the important. Many people never do the important—only the necessary. Here is a housewife whose life has no content. She arises in the morning, prepares breakfast, goes to the store, cleans the house, and on and on.

Here is another housewife who does precisely the same things, but her life has content and meaning. She is not faking it. She has given herself to God, and she has found a joy in giving herself for the sake of the beloved. She has learned the joy of pleasing her family—the joy there is in a clean house—for her life has a purpose and content. She listens for the cries of others; in her own way she becomes involved in their despair. She is for real.

You can apply this to businessmen, farmers, or men in the professions— it doesn't matter. But those who are seeking to be servants of others insofar as they can be brothers to them are few and far between. The man, the real man, who has service as his purpose in life, because he is ingrafted with Christ, is a rarity.

This is why the new you is so vitally important to the world. It is dying because it is unreal and fake, and beneath the slick veneer dry rot has spread far and wide. People who have had their blindness healed and who have faced up to reality and become ingrafted with Christ are its hope. *You* are the hope of the world when your life has this content. Don't ever sell yourself short!

The beginning place of content is always right at home. Wives, in the morning before your husband leaves for work, send him off with a song in his heart. Try giving him a real, genuine kiss of love. I don't mean one of those little skin-touchers or egg-wipers; I mean one which is for real. If he doesn't have a heart attack, he'll probably do the best day's work he's done in weeks.

Husbands, take a minute tomorrow and no matter how bumbling and haltingly, try telling your wife what she really means to you and how you appreciate what she does for the family—and that you simply couldn't get along without her. Then get out of her path, she'll tear the house apart piece by piece for a man like that.

Teenagers, have you ever told your parents how proud you are of them and how you love them? It is pretty easy to take them for granted. Tomorrow, just once without being told, hang all your clothing back where it belongs and get your room in tiptop shape. Then ask them if there are ways that you can be of some real help to them. I promise you when they regain consciousness, they'll be prouder than ever to have you for their son or daughter.

Content. It has to begin at home and branch out from there. Just a smile at everyone who comes into your store, a compliment in the right place, a phone call of appreciation. Do something nice for someone who doesn't care for you. These things are the meat of life, they are content.

Keep your eyes on your fellow humans. Listen for their cries for help; become involved in their despair. Keep tied on to God with your quiet time, worship Him as a family—these are the things that put meat and meaning into life. Keep your eye on Christ. Measure all things by Him.

In another place I have told *The Parable of the Diamonds.**

---

*Arnold Prater, *More Parables From Life* (Grand Rapids. Zondervan Publishing House, 1969).

A group of medical doctors were in Europe on a guided tour. They visited in Rotterdam, Holland, and were taken through the work rooms of a great company which dealt only in diamonds.

In the display room they were shown models of all the great diamonds of the world, including those in the crown of the King of England and the famous Hope diamond.

In the cutting room they watched entranced as the master craftsman studied the raw diamonds. They were told that X-rays were taken of every diamond and that they were studied for days before it was determined at just what precise point the diamond was to be struck.

If an error in calculation was made the stone would shatter into a thousand pieces leaving only a fairly cheap dust.

From here the doctors went to the grinding and polishing sections. They watched as the fragments were placed in incredibly small machines where they were ground until they were exquisitely formed with many sides. Then they were polished in a laborious process that was tedious enough to try the patience of the strongest man.

At last they were taken into a room where there was only one man. This was the assessor. He was surrounded by dozens of trays of finished diamonds. His job was to sort them according to their value, and with his eyeglass he would carefully look at each diamond for several minutes, then he would place it in a tray marked with a certain price.

One of the doctors engaged the assessor in conversation. "Tell me, sir," he said, "How is it you can look all day at hundreds of diamonds without becoming confused? How do you maintain your sense of values?"

The assessor smiled, "It's very simple, friend," replied the assessor, and he held out his hand. On one finger he wore a fabulous diamond ring. Then he said, "The diamond in this ring is perfect. It has not a single flaw. And every half hour or so I put it under my eyeglass. The picture of the perfect diamond restores my sense of values!"

Keep your eye on Christ. Measure everything by Him and His way. For His way is never the phony. By Him you can measure life and find the flaws, the imperfections, the little unnoticed things that sap the sweetness from living, and sift them out.

So we have made these affirmations of faith in our quest for the life that is real. From the altars of our hearts we have said, "From here on my life shall have a purpose, from here on my life shall have content."

"Forgetting what lies behind, I press on." Now there is a final affirmation I invite you to make with me: "From here on, I will constantly *look for God at work in his world.*"

There is nothing that differentiates the phony life from that which is real any more sharply than this. The phony believes in God, but he believes God is a kind of far-off creator who doesn't matter very much in the everyday affairs of men, who only comes down when the mortgage is about to be foreclosed or the baby dies. But the life that is for real believes that the Holy Spirit is at work in His world and constantly seeks to be aware of God's work among people.

By faith you can believe this. By faith you can know this. My glimpses of his workings have been too obvious and too real for me to doubt. Our need now is to grow and develop further *awareness* of His activity. We have begun to learn how to be aware of the cries of other people; now we seek further awareness of the workings of God in the lives of others.

I believe in the Holy Spirit, the active Presence of God in the world and in our lives. But one can never prove it scientifically. If there is any one group of people for whom I feel truly sorry it is the people who go through life constantly saying, "I must have proof. Intellectual proof. Take me to the laboratory."

I feel earnestly sorry for the people whose chief delight in life (many times used as a cover-up for disobedience) lies in splitting hairs or debunking something. The man who gets pleasure in telling you that after all Jesus wasn't born on December 25th is a pitiable creature. Those who want incessantly to argue about some peripheral little something that doesn't amount to a hill of beans and who utterly ignore the great Centrality are deeply in need. You may take faith out of religion and have some kind of religion left, but it won't be Christianity.

I believe that "chance" meetings, events, and opportunities are not always that at all, but sometimes the clear workings of God trying to get at the lives of people.

Some time ago I went over to the hospital and prayed silently as I entered it, "Lord, use me here." I had not gone fifty feet down the hall when a woman called my name. I went into her room. I had never seen her before, but she knew me. It developed that she had a desperate need and through prayer that need was met.

I could never prove scientifically that this "chance" meeting was not mere chance. But in the life that is for real, one is liberated from the necessity of needing proof for things like this. I believe the Holy Spirit of God directed that meeting. If He is concerned enough to watch the fall of a little sparrow to the earth, He surely was vitally concerned with the needs of that woman.

Some of you who are reading this may believe that you stumbled onto these pages by chance. Perhaps you did. But do not discount the possibility that maybe it was the leading of God and that in this way He is seeking to meet a need you have had for a long time.

In the life that is new and for real, in the life that is ingrafted with Christ, we *look* for God at work in our lives and in the lives of our brothers.

During the very days in which I have been writing these pages a letter came from a young man down in Texas. Two years ago I had preached for a week in a church he attended. With his permission, let me quote a very small portion of that letter:

> I really don't know how to put into words what I want to say here; through you God spoke in a way that still excites me when I think of it, for it was so personal and so directly to ME!
>
> On Tuesday night, you said that you were going to preach a sermon that was not the one you had prepared for this service, but that God had told you to bring a different message. You said that you felt this was intended for someone in the congregation that night. Brother Prater, I sat there and heard you ask questions that I had thought of but had been afraid to face. Your sermon that night was a personal message to me.

He went on to tell how he had surrendered to the call to the ministry and told something of his plans for the future.

The last thing I want to do is set myself up as an example, for God knows how far I have yet to go. Still, we must not hesitate to give credit to Him.

What if I had not trusted the leading of my heart that night? Two years passed before I knew what had happened. How many times have you listened to His leading and *never* known the results? This is why I am inviting you to make the affirmation to look for God at work in His world.

We could never prove that the Holy Presence had anything to do with my changing the sermon that night, but, let me repeat, it is wonderful to be freed from the necessity of the proof of the test tube and the slide rule.

These personal experiences are given only because they are not second-handed. They are not theories one has read in a book, they are happenings that have been lived out. God doesn't always show Himself so clearly, but He does it just often enough to shore up and fix fast our faith.

Some time ago I boarded a jet plane to go to Washington, D. C., for a preaching engagement at a minister's retreat in Virginia. I just happened to sit down by a certain man—or did it "just happen?"

This man turned out to be a salesman. He was definitely an extrovert—very loud, very confident, and very phony. He had a big cigar in his mouth and a large diamond on his finger. He wore alligator leather shoes and an obviously expensive suit. We started talking and he began to tell me of his great success with his company and about his great sales record and promotions. He had a fine home in Philadelphia in a very exclusive section. He didn't come right out and say he was earning lots of money, but I got the message! Well, I let him finish with his conversational catharsis, and then, because I thought I heard a faint cry in all this, I began to peel back the layers of his soul, one by one. Many times a stranger will open the door far more quickly than a close friend. Finally we got down to the bottom of things where he really lived and he wearily pulled off his mask. I found a great, raw wound down there—still bleeding.

He and his wife had no children. But years ago they

had had a little boy. One day disease struck and in a short time the little fellow was snatched away. When I heard his story I began gently to tell him of the healing and the love which God had for him.

I never could offer academic proof that the Holy Spirit, at work in the world, was in that meeting along the way. But the life that is for real has been cut loose from the bonds of material proof and soars in pure amazement and delight up in the great spaces of God's love and sees Him working still with the life and heart of every man.

There is never a week passes but that I do not view with reverence the *sustaining* power that God through Christ is pouring into the lives of people who have come to grips with reality. Every pastor sees the Word become flesh so often in the lives of his people that he goes from one awe-stricken experience to another.

If He will do it for them, He will surely do it for you when your testing comes. "They that wait upon the Lord shall renew their strength" is not simply Old Testament poetry. It is the most thrilling truth ever to explode into reality within a desperate heart.

A very dear minister friend of mine was pastor of a church in Virginia. He told me the story of Gloria. Gloria was a member of his congregation, and she sang in the church choir. She had a thrilling and lovely contralto voice. It was almost a tradition in that church that on Easter Sunday, just prior to the opening of worship, while that faint buzzing was still going on among the people, the organ would begin to play softly. Then Gloria, clad in a pure white robe, would come from the transept. She would walk to the center and enter the chancel, going up the steps to the very altar where she would turn and face the people. Then with the shine of heaven on her face she would begin to sing the heart-piercing melody of that grand old song of the Eastertime, "Open the Gates of the Temple."

Her voice would rise and swell, fade into softness and rise again until she came to the glorious, triumphant climax and she would sing:

> I know—I know—that my Redeemer liveth, And because
> he lives, I too shall live also!

Then the blessing of God would come down upon the people. For four years Gloria did this. She was the widowed mother of a small boy named Jimmie. When Jimmie was six years old he fell seriously ill with rheumatic fever. He recovered but it left him an invalid with a terribly damaged heart. For three years he was forced to stay in bed while the other boys ran and played. But as time passed the techniques for open heart surgery improved and it was decided to try it on Jimmie.

My friend had planned to go to the hospital that morning to be with Gloria. The newspapers had taken up the story and made a big thing of it. The entire area was watching and praying. About midnight the telephone rang; it was the doctor telling my friend that just a few minutes earlier, Jimmie's tired heart had just given up.

My friend hung up the receiver, dressed, and started across town to the hospital, all the while wondering what he could possibly say to Gloria. He took the elevator up to the sixth floor to the children's ward. He stepped out and started down the long hall towards Room 614. There was a hushed silence among the nurses and orderlies as they watched him pass.

He was about ten feet away when he heard a soft, low sounding coming from Room 614. It was Gloria, but she was not sobbing, she was *singing!*

He entered the room without saying a word. Gloria was going about the room, folding the little pajamas, picking up the comic books and the coloring games, and there was a kind of a radiance about her that no man could describe. My friend began to help her and to hum along with her as she softly sang—

> I know—I know—that my Redeemer liveth, And because he lives, I too shall live also . . .

When they had finished, he picked up her suitcase and took her by the arm. They went down the hall together, past the astonished doctors and nurses, down the elevator. Gloria was still singing. He put her in a taxicab and she sped off into the night—the blackest night of her life—but there was light—*everlasting light* in her soul!

> Man's life is laid in the loom of time,
>      to a pattern he does not see
> While the Weaver works and the shuttles fly,
>      'til the dawn of eternity.
> Not till the loom is silent and the shuttles
>      shall cease to fly,
> Shall God reveal the pattern—
>      and explain the reason why.

That is the faith on which the new you, released from phoniness, ingrafted with Christ, has risked everything.

But the outcome is no risk. Nothing has ever been more certain!

**Press on!**